Captain Ty Fatungase has been in commercial aviation for twenty-eight years, and has logged 12,000 hours of flying. He has flown the Fokker 27, Boeing 737, Airbus 310 and BAC 1-11. He is married and has two children. Presently, he is Managing Director and Chief Executive Officer of Air Meridian Ltd, Lagos, Nigeria.

Excerpts from the Sky

An Airline Pilot's Story

Excerpts from the Sky

An Airline Pilot's Story

Ty Fatungase

ATHENA PRESS
LONDON

ISBN 1 84401 562 9

Published 2006 by
ATHENA PRESS
Queen's House, 2 Holly Road
Twickenham TW1 4EG
United Kingdom

First published 1994

Printed for Athena Press

To my nuclear family,
Dele (my wife), Olushegun (first son),
and Olugbenga (second son),
who all painfully bore my parental detachment
during the compilation of this book

Acknowledgements

Captain A W O Williams, who never knew he was my inspiration from the beginning to the end of the book.

Captain Rabiu Aliyu for his moral and official support.

Captain Oluboyede whom I caused many sleepless nights.

Mr Peter Igbinedion – Executive Director, Okada Air Ltd.

Also my special thanks and profound gratitude to the ADC Airline management, that is, Captain Okon (CEO, ADC Airlines) Captain Udom, Captain Omame, Captain Alakija, Captain Akinkuotu, Captain Sandey and the rest of the "ADC clan" who took special personal and professional interest in the successful outcome of this publication.

Big thank you to Engineer Yinka Raji (CEO, Computer Concepts Ltd), Captain Rotimi Seriki, Mr Lekan Shote, Miss Mary Udoh (CCSL), Mr Segun Adesanya (Fadec Typesetting House), Nigeria Airways Computer Section Personnel, Mr ROC Chieke and my publishing manager Mr Shegun Adeleke aka "eleven o'clock", Mr Lucky Igbinedion and Mr Bright Igbinedion of Liman Bravo Mortgage Bank Ltd, and Mr Fadire of Okada Air Ltd.

To all those other numerous contributors to this publication I say thank you and God bless.

Lastly I thank Mr Tope Sanya Adeyinka (CEO, Tango Bravo & Associates) who supplied the book's title *Excerpts from the Sky*.

Foreword

I feel deeply honoured to be called upon by Captain Taiwo Fatungase to write the Foreword to his book *Excerpts from the Sky*.

Captain Taiwo Fatungase has indeed with this publication blazed the trail in the Nigerian aviation industry by being the first Nigerian airline pilot to write and publish a book on the technical aspects of piloting, and going further to simplify the topic by drawing from his personal experiences endeavouring as much as possible to simplify the topic by being just himself in his narration of the experience.

Since the incorporation of Nigeria Airways first as the West African Airways Corporation on the 23rd of August, 1958, as well as the growth in the number of private domestic airlines in Nigeria, the piloting profession had been in need of enlightenment in the form of this publication, as the piloting profession has been misunderstood in terms of functions, substance of academic requirements of the profession, and derided, as to leadership and management capabilities of the individual pilot. This book has made a great effort to clear the air in these regards.

The book touches on a lot of legal and technical aspects of not only piloting but flying, and the author has tried his best to simplify these issues as much as possible for the green mind, without compromising details in any respect in the case of the already familiar mind seeking to both refresh and further enrich its mental library.

The book is at its best consumer material as well as educational material for would-be pilots and others interested in flying. It is also a useful tool to pilots both young and old, the Aviation Regulatory Authority, the airlines, and most importantly, the passengers.

Anthony T Laleye Esq. (LL.M. PG Dip Air & Space Law, B.L.)
Air & Space Law Practitioner,
Lagos, Nigeria.

Contents

Introduction   xiii

Is this Flying?   17

My Experience in Flying   24

Life Before Flight School   36

Almost There   47

The Zaria Experience and the Making

      of a Productive Second Officer   64

The Making of a First Officer   76

Boeing my Way   126

The Good Life   180

Glossary   197

BAC 1–11 Aircraft. Courtesy: ADC Airline

Introduction

Excerpts from the Sky was born out of my burning desire to inform society about the thrills of the aviation industry, with emphasis on the airlines vis-à-vis flight execution and passenger carriage. Compilations in this book have been centred upon the African aviation industry mostly, with Nigeria Airways as the central focus.

Also, the contents of the book consist mainly of my personal experience, a wellspring of information obtained from my active flight line duties as a Nigeria Airways pilot spanning fourteen years.

Most of the details are facts, and comments that could lead to further discourse are welcome. I have tried as much as humanly possible to convey my message clearly, and it is hoped that the reader will find this book both educational and entertaining.

Getting Airborne

The number of operating African airlines may be determined by taking a roll-call of all the sovereign states on the African continent. The fad of naming an airline after one's country makes the task easier. The major airlines in Africa include those belonging to countries like Ghana, Ethiopia, Nigeria, Uganda, Kenya, Gabon, Egypt, Libya and Senegal, to mention a few. The moment you add the prefix Air or Airline to these names, then you have named an airline. This was the trend when African nations started establishing national airlines. This trend started from 1940.

But before this, air transportation had been around to serve and satisfy the greed and the supposed treasure-hunting activities of the colonial powers for the vast and untapped African mineral resources including gold, copper and uranium. It was not a great surprise then that when gold deposits were discovered in the African Guinea, an airline was easily conceived there. This became the genesis of massive air transportation of cargo from the African soil. The subsequent shift in emphasis from cargo, which ostensibly was the main objective of the pioneer colonial air transportations, to passenger carriage may be attributed to the simple and logical fact that education (being the primary and vital vehicle of civilisation) was gaining ground fast in the African societies. With this development, travelling by air was just a matter of time for the now-enlightened African public.

The first form of aeroplane was the DC3, generally referred to as the Dakota. It had a twin-prop piston engine and was a very ugly piece of equipment, but, incidentally, Second World War pilots regarded it as a marvel. This ugly piece of metal however proved reliable and flew satisfactorily. And much to the joy of the colonialists, it also defied the brazen and scorching heat of the African tropics. These aircraft were operated all around Africa from the 1930s to the late 1960s, even after the advent of the jet airplane in the early '50s and '60s. It is necessary to mention that the DC3 was not the only aircraft used during this period. Other aircraft like the Pussmoth and the Piper cub formed part of the colonial airplane fleet.

Colonial air transportation in Africa cannot be strictly said to have started in all parts of the continent at the same time because some African nations like Egypt and Ethiopia had started their own national airlines as far back as 1932, with Egypt Air as the oldest African airline. It was formed in 1932 as MIS Airwork and was renamed United Arab Airline in 1960. Its formation was unique in the sense that the workforce was enviously indigenous, unlike most other African airlines that were incorporated solely to serve colonial ventures and for imperialistic reasons. Today, most, if not all, African airlines are state-owned.

Carriage of passengers by airlines in Africa started in the 1940s and African airlines have carried, cumulatively, millions of passengers to date. Today, they can boast of numerous and different aircraft types that form their fleet. Airplanes like the B737, B747, B767, DC10, F27 and BACl-11 are now a common sight in numerous airfields all over the African continent.

The development of these mostly state-owned airlines has played a major and dynamic role in the areas of economic growth, social transformation and cultural revival in many African states in recent times. The vital role these state-owned airlines play in promoting solidarity amongst sovereign African states and also restoring peace between some warring states cannot be overemphasised.

Airline structures globally are relatively similar to one another. All profit-oriented airlines need to fulfil the two basic and mandatory requirements of acquiring adequate equipment and manpower. Since a strong financial base is required in order to be able to purchase the highly expensive and vital equipment needed for any airline to be operationally viable, most of the early airlines on the continent were state-owned. However, today, in Nigeria, there are quite a few privately-owned airlines. In recent times, state-owned and privately-owned airlines alike have been able to improve their financial base, thereby enhancing their ability to purchase vital equipment. But one major problem being faced every day is that of manpower and the attitude of the contemporary African worker in the technologically sophisticated aviation industry. Ineptitude has become a major feature of much needed indigenous hands. The consequence of this is throwing away large sums of hard currency in employing the sometimes dubious expatriates. This sordid situation is however gradually changing for the better due to the greater emphasis now being placed on continuous and rigorous training of the indigenous hands.

Since it will be quite futile writing details about each and every airline of African origin in service today, I have chosen Nigeria Airways as a case study. Nigeria Airways is the fastest growing African airline and almost the biggest airline on the continent. Thus, the airline made available a greater volume of information than any other airline in compiling this book. Suffice it to say that this is so, considering the fact that her indigenous-cum-operational workforce is well over 98% of total staff strength which is far more impressive than what obtains in most other African airlines.

Is this Flying?

Only birds have in them the inherent ability to get airborne or, in common parlance, to fly. Their natural ability and perfection in flight has always impressed man, who marvels at the beautiful grace with which birds flock the sky, looking down probably in superior amusement at the other inhabitants of the planet Earth of which man is not only a major part, but also the paramount settler.

The awe of man for this natural feat of birds soon turned to envy, which in turn triggered the efforts of the progenitors of aviation to set out in search of ways to conquer outer space. In their strong commitment to achieving this goal, men were known to have fixed on their shoulders feathers from birds to try to get airborne. All such attempts, however, turned out to be unsuccessful. But with continuous sacrifice, dedication, and the strong resolve to overcome this challenge, man finally found a way to realise his ambition. This came about with the invention of the "iron bird", which Nostradamus saw in one of his legendary visions. The "iron bird" is the airplane.

The advent of the airplane was a big technological breakthrough. But the euphoria that followed this remarkable achievement was short-lived. The aircraft got airborne but soon faced unexpected handicaps, namely weather, airplane component failure, turbulence and crew fatigue, which sometimes led to crew phobia during the duties.

Most cockpit crew to date have suffered from phobia in the line of duty induced by thunderstorms, component failure, and so on, simply because of the natural instinct of self-preservation. Nor is their phobia uncalled for, for these two flight hazards, among so many others not mentioned yet, have led to the deaths of many in numerous plane crashes.

An opinion poll carried out in 1977 in the USA voted the airline pilot as the third most glamorous job in the USA. As for me, after fourteen years as an airline pilot, I still fail to see where this glamour lies. Glamour should be blissful, and not a mixed grill of fear, anxiety, and the nightmare of the unknown. My candid opinion is that this is certainly not the graceful type of flying enjoyed by birds but a deliberate and reasonably high risk taken because of a latent curiosity to discover the unknown, and my childhood fascination with what it would be like to get airborne. The task of realising my childhood fantasy in this regard is portrayed as we go on in this book, with the most emphasis on my personal encounters and experiences during the active period of my airline career both as co-pilot and later captain, which has today spanned fourteen years.

The Story in a Blitz

I got initiated into the aviation world through the flight training school in January 1977. This was the year I started getting the bromide of the vast and thoroughly established world of aviation. This is so because in the school environment one was able to get naturally an insight into the global trend of the aviation industry, with special emphasis on commercial airline operation, flight execution, and the laws and regulations guiding the operation of commercial aviation.

In trying to achieve a near 100% safety level in day-to-day flight operation, aviation research has over the years been accorded great importance. To do otherwise would amount to taking an additional risk in an already risky profession.

Let us take, for example, the case of weather. Weather phenomena are transient in nature and unpredictable. At the onset of aviation, weather constituted a major headache. But through intensive research, meteorological experts have been able to achieve about 65% accuracy in weather forecasts. As research in this area continues, there is hope that some day absolute certainty will be achieved in weather forecasts, using very sensitive equipment that has been developed and is still being developed.

Summing up the bizarre character of weather among other problems of the aviation industry forces me to ask again the question that is the title of this chapter: "Is this Flying?" Well, the answer equipment-wise, is an emphatic *yes*. But my natural and candid answer is a reluctant *no*. Why? The harsh realities of the odds faced on almost a daily basis in the line of aviation duty will unfold in subsequent chapters, backing my honest answer.

For now, let all passengers purchase tickets to their different destinations, collect their boarding passes and wait for boarding announcements.

I joined the airline, Nigeria Airways, as one of nine success-ful candidates after a highly competitive selection process. I was so ecstatic about this feat I had just performed, only to discover sadly that I had just worked hard to get myself into a company that boasted of a workers' loop that had the stigma of possessing the most politicised work climate. My first physical encounter in this regard came in the process of being integrated into the company's mainstream. First, I was posted to the dispatch office of the company's operations department. Given the comedy of organised disorganisation and naked confusion in the outfit regarding its perennial custom of no real or well-defined job format or description for any newly employed pilot, reporting for duty at this office was like reporting for duty at an architec-tural or law firm because you are completely at a loss on arrival. The proper place for a pilot is the cockpit of an airplane.

Although the dispatch office is an integral part of flight operations, it has never been part of a pilot's job description or format. So, a pilot reporting here for duty is a classic case of "No business as usual, idleness and immediate redundancy". This shocking beginning for me lasted for seven months and ended when I was finally sent to Nigeria's equivalent of the Oxford Flight Institute, Kidlington England, known as the Nigerian Civil Aviation Institute, Zaria, for further assessment as a pilot. This was necessary because as a rookie pilot, I was certificated in the USA. Emphasis during assessment was principally based not surprisingly on the Oxford syllabus, which (when compared to the American syllabus) really was an amplified version of the basic American flight training. In brief, the training programme turned out to be another academic exploit in civil aviation. Well, the solace was that "no knowledge is a waste". On the successful completion of the course, I was sent back to Lagos to keep faith and wait for the airplane type conversion course.

After a few weeks of waiting on arrival from the Zaria Institute (which was supposedly an assessment graveyard for the majority of the graduate pilots from American flight institutes), I now appeared in ground school to undergo a systems course of the aircraft I was about to fly on the fleet I had been selected for. It was the Fokker Friendship F27 aircraft. It was only then that I began to feel that after all I was going to become an airline pilot. This was because for the first time since I joined this outfit, a long-time serving hand, our ground school instructor, bestowed on us exceptional hospitality, both in his style of teaching new (but now timid) intakes, and his personal relations. The gentleman was very humble and full of advice and admiration for our making it to the class against all odds. This had the effect of boosting the ego after the long traumatic disorder of the integration process. After a few weeks, ground school was over. The civil aviation authority examination was taken and passed, and in a jiffy this time around we got scheduled for the real event: flying.

For aircraft-type rating base training (as it is called) nine of us, divided into different training groups, proceeded to Port Harcourt. On seeing the training schedule, I realised I had arrived days ahead of my scheduled date. So I joined the group before mine to get acquainted and ready for my scheduled date.

The group trained under Captain Valerio, who was the instructor (flight). The instructor put into play the usual custom of being elusive, thereby making himself a scarce treasure to hunt for. In the end, he emerged from the unknown and surveyed the training bunch like the mother hen sizing up her chicks about to learn the art of flying.

This time around the "birds" were big; not those kite-like trainer airplanes in the flight training schools. He knew what sermon to preach to the rookies for the sake of first impression in accordance with the textbook rules on the art of flight instruction. First, he got down to the real business for about one and a half hours. Then he did a procedure turn and commenced the standard instructor/student hogwash, getting very pedantic about F27 aircraft to convince the students that he was present at the aircraft's assembly line.

Well before this sermon at our hotel accommodation, some dual professionals (fliers and tale tellers) had started sounding off about the beauty of the school they had attended, and their aeronautic escapades while there. The tales were so off the cuff that at a point I believed them to be about boats and ships and certainly not about aircraft. Some spoke of record achievements that would make certain entries about aircraft flying in the *Guinness Book of Records* look ordinary to say the least. There was this guy who did everything he could to achieve group hegemony for some reasons best known to him, but who finally did himself in while narrating a story about the use of a component installed in a jet aircraft (which he claimed he had flown), called the "Reversers". This lever-type mechanism is used in jet airplanes on the ground during landing roll to deflect the flow of air from the engine's exhaust nozzle, in a forward direction. This reverse thrust results in a braking action on ground for the airplane. The reverse was the case as told by this chap, who claimed that he had times without number used this ground operated mechanism to reverse his aircraft in the air any time the situation called for it. Of course, anybody with the faintest idea of flying would know that this is impossible, and such a claim was bizarre coming from a pilot. This particular trainee simply portrayed himself as nothing but a charlatan, that ilk to be found the world over in all professions. He made so much fuss about everything and anything to do with the training programme that he achieved the self-abnegation of not boarding the aircraft, not to speak of training at all.

Now back to the commander-in-chief of the training and demi-god, who was from the Philippines. After he had ended his sermon in Port Harcourt, I put all the useful points I had gathered from his Filipino-accented sermon in my memory box and tossed the negative bonus rhetoric to my charlatan friend who relished all.

The training itself (for this first group) turned out to be a case of three green pilots trying so hard and innocently to achieve self-destruction and the felony of manslaughter in respect of others on the plane by committing some near-fatal flight errors. The airplane's size, and her relatively high speed maze, came to be a problem that could have got us all killed if not for the virtuous skill and the Red Army-type alertness of the instructor. At a point, the blunders became quite alarming and the whole training programme would have ended in a fiasco.

Well, in the end with a lot of practice, the group got through. As for me, I had played an observer role all the time. My presence in the airplane throughout the group's training had been unofficial. I was in the third group and my group's turn for training was two weeks after this first group had finished. However, my pre-emptive and illegal resolve to observe group one's training revealed a lot to me regarding what I would be facing later myself. In the end, I got trained and then I finally got confirmed as a second officer on the F27 fleet.

Now as second officer, I reported for duty for the first time in the real world of flying. At last, I got my deserved respect from the dispatcher, who followed the right procedure of serving his senior officer. While I was waiting for the rest of the technical crew in the dispatch office, the co-pilot for the flight appeared. Luckily, he turned out to be a pleasant and amiable fellow. He took his time while being briefed about the flight he had shown up for. He knew already from his roster that he had a second officer coming along on the flight too, so he looked for a strange face on the flight line wearing the rank of a second officer. Then we made contact and methodically, he started giving me a scintilla of what to expect of the flight and of the captain. Suddenly, the arrival of the captain was signalled by a behavioural change amongst the dispatchers. The captain wasted no time in getting down to business. You could see easily from his face and conduct the changes he must have gone through so far during his long years of experience. He beckoned to the first officer to get closer to him while he took his briefing, after which they now jointly compared notes before he finally put his signature on the briefing paper. He soon got to know about the rookie coming along with him and I introduced myself to him. He did not mince words in telling me about his dos and don'ts once the job got under way. His conversation with me was strictly formal and official and he then went into a speech about the seriousness of career flying and ended the whole sermon by wishing me the best of luck.

We got to the airplane, did the pre-flight check and held a brief discussion with the aircraft maintenance engineer on duty after which the passengers were called to board. Passengers got boarded, and – boom! – we were on our way. Not long after getting airborne, the captain pushed the call button in response to which appeared the unquestionable manifestation of beauty – a stewardess who now stood behind us with rapt attention. She announced her presence and all of a sudden, our earlier all-prim-and-proper serious man of a captain dropped his boss-like, I'm-in-charge mask, softened up and asked the stewardess for a kiss – which he got too! Then he asked her in a well-tailored and romantically commanding tone for his breakfast. The request was immediately acknowledged, and she asked the first officer if he too wanted his breakfast. Having got his response, she walked away from the cockpit, oblivious of the second officer's presence.

She came back, served breakfast for two as requested, then turned round to inform me in pidgin English that the Catering Department had no provision of meals for me through the duration of the flight. I wondered about the truth of her state-ment but soon found out, much to my annoyance, that denial of meals was the traditional price that must be paid to the cabin attendant for being new on the flight line.

The rookie second officer did a lot of paying in so many other ways, and pretty soon, he too wanted to know whether indeed this was *flying*.

My Experience in Flying

I started active flight engagement with Nigeria Airways on the 21st of August, 1980, under the command of Captain Ogunaike, at which time I was a trainee pilot on the Fokker Friendship F27 turboprop aircraft. I remember vividly the aircraft registration, which was 5N-ANS. The other trainees in my training group were second officers Bonojo, Ikpeme and Agboso. I realised during the type rating training (as it is known in aviation) that official red-tapism had eaten into the fabric of all units and groups, which ideally should have been united to achieve an efficient workforce. Consequently, there was poor coordination among all units involved in the training, including the flight operations department, the engineering and maintenance department and even the central control department. This prolonged the training period. To have an airplane type rating endorsed on a pilot's licence, he is required by law to have successfully gone through the airplane training programme. This programme from my personal experience of having gone through three different fleets in Nigeria Airways, namely the F27, the B737 and the A310 airbus in that order, was a repetitive and amusing theatrical display of how things can go wrong while the cast think they have laboured hard to make them go the right way. Why? Because to train one needs an aircraft, a training instructor, the trainees and then the other support units I have earlier mentioned. Well, the comedy began from the manner in which the instructor and his trainees got informed on a daily basis about the training schedule.

Sometimes, it turned out that the instructor was aware of a training schedule but the trainees were not, and sometimes the reverse was the case. Then, when both parties were in the know, it often turned out that there was no aircraft available, or that the one available had no fuel in it. There were days when everything seemed to be in order but the weather was not suitable for training purposes. Also, quite often, getting the airplane scheduled was hindered by official preference for 100% airplane utilisation for passenger service rather than for training purposes since training was non-revenue generating. When this became persistent, the pilots had to lobby for the provision of an aircraft for training.

Although the whole scenario sounds funny and unreal, these were the true events that transpired during aircraft training in Nigeria Airways. With these institutionalised problems, training duration for different training groups depended largely on fate and sometimes on the complex web of personal connection in the company's management cadre.

How I Got There

What paved the way to my becoming an airline pilot was my childhood fascination with airplanes, which in turn resulted from living in an airport environment. Each day as a boy, I watched with keen interest and admiration the take-off and landing of airplanes.

I was born along with a twin sister, into the family of Mr and Mrs S O Fatungase on the 26th of June, 1958 at University College Hospital in the city of Ibadan, capital of the then Western Region of Nigeria. The family lived in the aerodrome area of the city.

My parents' nuclear family is made up of six children, four males and two females, of whom I am either the third or fourth, depending on the perspective. Following western logic my coming into the world one hour ahead of my twin sister makes me the third child of the family. But this is not so from my native (Yoruba) traditional perspective.

By Yoruba tradition, it is the *second* twin to arrive that is regarded as the senior. The logic is that the second tot actually sent the first to go and taste the world first, hence the name, *To-aye-wo*, shortened to *Taiye*. This too is believed to be the oracle's verdict, which is final in Yoruba tradition. Our family in the then societal context, was relatively middle class. My father was a legal practitioner and his wife (my mother, now deceased) was a qualified nurse who later on became a household name as a successful trader in Ibadan city.

As a child, I attended the kindergarten school of Alafia Institute in the Mokola area of Ibadan between 1962 and 1963. I then went on to attend ICC Primary School in the same Mokola district between 1964 and 1967 for the initial part of my elementary school education. I later proceeded to Ebenezer African Church Primary School in 1968, and there I gained admission to a secondary school in the 1970 academic year. Since my elementary education had been nomadic in nature, it was only natural to envisage the same during my secondary education too.

Initially, I attended Iwo Baptist High School from 1970 to 1971, and then transferred to the Government College, Ibadan, where I finally wrote my West African School Certificate Examination in 1974.

On leaving secondary school in 1974, the onus was on me to either follow the academic fad of proceeding to university or going ahead to actualise my childhood dream of becoming a pilot. Having been blessed with educated parents, achieving the former goal would be easy enough, but I needed no diviner to tell me that my desire to become a pilot could be abhorrent to my parents, who preferred academic achievements to professional training. So I had to suspend the announcement of my decision and instead continuously wrote concessional entrance examinations to different universities in the country between 1974 and 1976. After a two-year period of subterfuge to set the stage, I took the next step of capitalising on my parents' now waning confidence in my academic ability and informed them that I wanted to become an aviator.

Their answer predictably, was an emphatic *no*. As I insisted, it was made clear to me what the situation was: I was on my own and good luck. But I refused to be deterred. I had a dream even as a child and although it was like a fantasy, I had come to accept the dream as my future and my life, no matter the problems that might be involved. My ignorance at the time of the existence of a flight training school in Nigeria left me with the painful choice of leaving the country for any school offering flight training courses for beginners. Knowledge of the existence of the flight school in

Zaria would have greatly mitigated the thorny path I trod in achieving my set goal. In 1975, when I was only seventeen years old, I had to leave the shores of Nigeria like the "Andrews" of the late 1980s checking out, except that an Andrew was an older and seemingly defeated soul overreacting to the problems of his developing country and believing the only solution was to run away from his fatherland to another country. In my own case, I was far from a defeated soul fleeing from the complex problems of the nation's Third World economy. I was just naturally reaching out to achieve my goal in life. I was alone and had fallen out with my parents who were my only benefactors. I was only being as obstinate as any innocent young man with a dream. In addition to the challenge posed by my parents' stance, other odds against me came in the form of difficulties in raising funds to finance my trip and in processing international travel documents.

Raising the Capital

The only way I knew of making money when I was seventeen was to get a job. At least, this way, one was sure of eventually building up some honest savings some day, enough to take care of the financial barrier between me and my aspiration.

In trying to get a job, I registered at the Federal Ministry of Labour, Department for the Unemployed, then situated in the Ekotedo Iyaolobe area of Ibadan. The method of registering was simply appearing at the premises of the three-storey building and just entering your name in a big worn-out book called a register. Well, the book might have been old and worn out, but the order of names was strictly followed whenever there was a vacancy in any government parastatal. The routine was to report at this building every morning and hope for an opening somewhere. My opportunity came at last towards the end of 1975 when I was sent from the labour department to attend an interview at the Federal Ministry of Forestry in Ibadan for the post of library assistant. At least there was the chance of making money if my interview was successful. I was elated at the welcome news and prepared hard for the interview. Thank God

I did not get carried away by any presumption that being sent from the government employment agency gave one an edge over other applicants.

The interview venue turned out to be a colourful festival of the unemployed from far and wide. There were well over three hundred job seekers, male and female alike; three hundred vying for the single post of library assistant. The large gathering led to a beehive of activity and amusing side attractions. For one thing, it turned out to be the biggest suit and tie festival I had ever witnessed. On parade there were suits of different cuts and styles, complemented by ties of amazing lengths and widths. Then there was the skirt and blouse parade. It was the usual parade of long and short skirts with the long reflecting the serious and religious females, while the short showed the opposite. The number of applicants for just this single position caused me a little bit of anxiety. Well, the elimination process got under way, and within the twinkle of an eye we had surprisingly shrunk to thirty-five candidates after the first routine of having all applicants' certificates scrutinised. This spiral dive from over three hundred applicants to thirty-five has continued to be a source of amusement to me till today.

The next phase for the rest of us was to now demonstrate our knowledge of the English language by writing a composition on why we wanted to work with the Federal Ministry of Forestry, and in particular why we wanted to become library assistants. Although I remember making a beautiful presentation of my reasons in order to secure the post, the bottom line was simply that I needed funds for my travel plans. The thirty-five of us submitted our essays and an hour later, seven of us were asked to stay behind, while the rest were dismissed. All the interview activities so far had been conducted in an open space, and from 12.00 p.m. it became so hot that, remembering much later, it was easy to appreciate the message in the reggae album of the Third World which sang the track "96 Degrees Centigrade in the Shade".

At last, the remaining seven of us got the first glint of hospitality in a government parastatal by eventually being invited into this well-air-conditioned conference room where a panel of judges to handle the next phase of the elimination process was already waiting. This time, it was a general debate. After twenty minutes of panel/applicant exchange of views on current affairs, five other guys joined the rest of the earlier acquitted bunch. Now came the final stage, at which the other chap excelled. He was pronounced the lucky applicant and, with a heavy heart, I went home feeling very tired and disappointed. I had run a hard race only to end up the runner-up.

But who says there's no God? Surprisingly, two weeks later I got a letter from the Federal Ministry of Forestry inviting me to come and assume duty as assistant librarian. My conqueror had got a better offer somewhere else and so had turned down the post. There is a miracle in being number two sometimes. So I started work. It was the first job in my life so far. My office was not a bad place at all, I worked with a bunch of nice people and the work climate was very conducive for my plans too. I came to realise that some of my colleagues were planning to head for the United Kingdom to continue their earlier aborted academic pursuits. So the office turned out to be a small clan of goal-seeking travellers. The beauty was in our being able to compare our travelling notes now and then. My enthusiasm around the office ebbed though, when I suddenly realised that bureaucracy was going to lead to my waiting three months before collecting my first earnings as an employee. The waiting period was a bit of a setback to my planned departure although I had not set a departure date. My net pay came to about N99.00k per month. As soon as I got paid my three months' salary in a lump sum, I was out of that office like a bat out of hell. As far as raising funds for the trip was concerned, my mission was accomplished. While at the Ministry, I had made the necessary arrangements to secure my international travelling passport.

The Passport Debacle

Towards the end of 1975, I took a trip to the passport office in Ibadan in the then Ring Road area of Ibadan precinct (the road is now known as Ibrahim Babangida Road), to seek information about how to go about obtaining an international passport. The procedure, I was told, was to collect an application form after paying a fee of N06.00k but how to correctly fill in the form with the requested information remained your own responsibility. The joy of having collected the form disappeared immediately when I looked through the whole information format. Simply put, it was a nightmare for any seventeen-year-old kid trying to do it alone. Considering the information required one could easily describe the process as the case of one's chosen guarantor going into a nexus-type contract with one's chosen guardian, with the passport officer as the solicitor and advocate.

Finding a guarantor and then a guardian was a big headache for me. I just didn't have a clue. The going had now got tough, so the tough had to get going. It was now my show, so I had no other choice than to approach and pay some faceless figures to stand in as my guarantor and guardian respectively. I learnt this ploy from the passport office grapevine department of counselling for handicapped applicants. That took care of that problem. The form got completed and was submitted for onward dispatch to the headquarters in Lagos. The next phase was now the waiting game – waiting for the collection of the passport. My near-pauper status resulting in my not being able to afford tips to the passport office wise guys, causing me a continuous pilgrimage of almost a year to that office enquiring about the arrival of my passport from the headquarters in Lagos. "This needn't have taken so long," enthused one of the wise guys on the day I finally collected the document. But now I had in my possession a passport at last.

The Ticket and the Visa Scam

I purchased my ticket to travel through one of the numerous and well-informed travel agencies on Broad Street in Lagos. I did not get to this travel agency by chance; it was as a result of one of the numerous travel tips I had gathered from the little travelling clan at the Federal Ministry of Forestry. It turned out to be a worthwhile tip. This particular travel agency demonstrated consummate understanding of the vast needs of intending travellers. Their approach was very scientific. I still recall my own experience at their office. The moment I presented my passport for the purpose of purchasing an air ticket, and told them my destination as well as my travel plans, they immediately referred me to an appropriate official of theirs who advised me on how best to go about my journey. Without wasting time, I confided to the official my fears about being able to obtain a British visa. Since, by the agency's assessment, I was a highly needy would-be passenger, they decided that I should meet with the manager of the outfit. That decision of theirs gave some hope, until I found out that the manager was a friend of my parents. The meeting was no longer interesting for me because of this discovery. The manager wanted to know if I had the consent of my parents regarding my trip. I was too dumb to respond to this question. The manager, I reasoned, should know that if I had my parents' consent I would not be sitting in front of him and seeking professional assistance.

He knew my family all right, but he just saw no harm in pulling my leg all the same. The man was liberal and did his best to solve my problem. With his wealth of experience, he was able to come up with a suggestion that solved what I had earlier considered an insurmountable problem. The suggestion, which I promptly carried out, was to pay N350.00k for an excursion ticket of Nigeria Airways. With this, I was routed from Lagos through Heathrow Airport, London, for a brief overnight stop, which, due to the arrival time of the Nigeria Airways flight I would be catching, left me with the only option of continuing my trip to my final destination (Paris) the next day by joining Air France. Since (as a decoy) I had made Paris my final destination, the agency only charged me the going fee of N07.00k for the procurement of a French visa. The agency issued me a ticket and also returned my passport stamped with a three-month French visa.

On collection of my passport, I was reminded by the manager of the need to avoid any form of panic on getting to the entry point in London, which happened to be my real destination. The ball was now in my court to make whatever I could of the game plan. The agency had done the best it could for me and I was determined not to let myself down.

I now had my passport, flight ticket, French visa (that I would be trading verbally with in place of a British visa) and, in hard coins and not currency, forty British pence, which was all the money I had.

At last the departure day came. Only my twin sister was around to see me off. Just as she did the day we were born, she was again seeing me off ahead of herself once more to go and survey the terrain before she arrived later in the UK to join me. What a drag! I am always her fall guy, but I love it too. There is always a price to pay for arriving early at an event. That was my reward for being her natural fall guy, so to speak.

Checking Out

On my departure date, the 26th of July 1976, my material assets other than my travelling papers were two shirts, two pairs of trousers and two pairs of shoes, and these formed the contents of my one-piece luggage. The airport as usual was a hive of activity. Pain was the watchword in the process of finally boarding the Nigeria Airways flight WT 800. The trip to London was uneventful. After flying six and a half hours, we arrived at Heathrow Airport, London. The B707 airplane parked and we got deplaned. We had instructions from the airport officials to proceed to the terminal three wing of the airport so as to go through immigration formalities. As I walked towards the immigration hall, I rehearsed in my mind the storyline I had for the immigration officials. I joined a long queue of other passengers waiting to be cleared at the immigration point. The immigration interview got to my turn, and to my utmost surprise, after passport presentation to an immigration official, he just asked me when I would like to continue my trip to Paris, and how long I would like to stay in the UK before proceeding. He then returned my passport to me, stamped with a six-,month leave to stay in the UK, if I so wished. If I so wish? What a big joke! I didn't need to be asked. I did so wish! As I walked past the immigration desk, it suddenly dawned on me that life was a carpet of odds that would continue to unfold till the end of time. Here was I a few minutes ago pondering how to overcome immigration problems. Then that got solved, and at once I was faced by another problem: the weather.

The weather that day in the month of August was chilly and harsh. Little did I know that the weather was a mirror of what would be coming up next in the name of survival. Tersely put, life became harsh. As I walked through the arrival hall that evening, emerging on the porch, I felt like a fish out of water. So many people were at the arrival lounge, waiting for their loved and hated ones alike. Remember, I had only one individual as my departure party so I certainly was not expecting any welcome party either. In the flurry of activity around the arrival lounge, I walked towards one of the phone booths and placed a call to a friend of mine who had no prior information concerning my arrival. The line turned out to be a wrong line. I tried reaching another friend, but it also ended up with the same response. Right there and then my whole money – forty pence – finished. I had become bankrupt within two hours of my arrival in the UK. Jesus! Did I feel lost? Yes, but only for a brief moment. Out of the blue, some hawk-eyed Nigerian chaps recognised, even in the stampeded lounge, the lost-in-transit look that I was now wearing, and, for reasons best known to them, they came to my aid. I didn't have to go into the story of my self-induced dilemma. Two chaps came towards me at first, then a few other guys joined us and they eventually formed a ring round me. Before I could even utter a word, they had all started chattering in my native Yoruba tongue. These chaps were very sympathetic and nice to me. I had a feeling that it was my complete innocence born out of being quite young then that earned me their sympathy. In a jiffy, they got me out of my bankruptcy through their generous donations, which added up to £68. I just couldn't believe this. Looking lost and innocent sure could be good business around the airport. The thought of exploiting that avenue could be quite tempting to any lazy ass. For me, I didn't come all the way to the UK to start begging. I came to achieve a goal, so whichever was the hard and right way, I was ready. I was young, determined and physically fit. I knew no vices of life then, not to speak of having taken part in any. I had come to face the world, and I was prepared for whatever came my way.

With my new status, and boasting £68 in my kitty, I set out for my friend's house, the one I had tried earlier on to reach on the phone. I hoped that it would not be a continuous case of the wrong number. My airport donors had advised me to go by public bus, which was the cheapest means of transportation. According to the address I sought, my journey was towards the eastern side of London. Although the fare was cheap, the long duration of the bus ride was a new experience altogether. Before I got on the bus, I had no idea of the number of the bus that was plying my route. I thought the route would be clearly indicated on the bus and so I waited at the bus stop, expecting the bus to arrive. The cold and harsh weather finally made me hop onto the next available bus, before I almost froze to death. The bus I got on was the right one to keep me alive, but turned out to be the wrong one for my journey. So the trip that should normally have taken under an hour lasted a whopping twenty-four hours. That was the penalty I had to pay coming from a country where destination announcements by bus conductors and touts were a guide for commuters. Though some municipal buses back home in Nigeria carried numbers on them too, I had never seen the numbers being put into use. Reliance on numbers rather than on touts was alien to me. I changed buses more than fifteen times before I finally arrived at my friend's doorstep shivering terribly. Thank God, it turned out to be the right address too. One thing about all disappointments which I have learnt is that latent in them is some form of blessing. My unplanned one-day bus trip became a tourist excursion around the city of London. I had carried out this tour without touching a penny of my kitty. The bus pass which had been part of my gift package from the airport chaps turned out to be like the American express card in public bus services and it took care of the tour.

When I changed buses I had some dramatic experiences as a result of the shoes I had on, which were platform shoes in vogue among youngsters in Nigeria then. To make matters worse, mine was a six-inch pair and shot me up from my natural height of 5' 9" to an artificial one of about 6' 3" which, of course, disastrously raised upward my centre of gravity. So during the few short walks between bus stops, with the road wet and slippery due to rain showers, I recorded no fewer than five body slams into the pavement. Every time I fell, I got so embarrassed and ashamed of myself because I knew that I had the wrong pair of shoes on. Too bad though, those were the only pair I had, so I had no choice but to wear them. I thanked God that at least I didn't break any bones. This would have simply added more to my already full sack of odds. I hate remembering those body slams. The effortless manner in which they were achieved would have made the pair of Gino Brito and Gino Bravo (the IBWA wrestlers) turn green with envy.

At last, I was united with my friend. He was surprised but not shocked to see me, and he took the surprise nicely. We had been classmates in the high school. Easily, we went into the mumbo jumbo of the time in high school and other stories about home for him to catch up on the latest news from there, with me countering with curiosity for "what's gwan?" in London. My friend didn't waste time in spelling out the reality of living and attending school in London. The bottom line in my case was to get a job first, and very fast too. Well, as for that, I was more than ready.

Life Before Flight School

London, here I come. The OYO (on your own) acronym was in action once more. My pal had done the little he could housing me temporarily. The rest was up to me. I didn't know the streets of London, but there was no law against wandering, neither did I see any form of discrimination against pedestrians. So I was completely free to traverse the streets of London in search of a job, although it was illegal for an immigrant in my category to do so. The British Home Office wouldn't take kindly to that. Well, I apologise to Her Majesty, the Queen of England (whose son, Prince Charles, I had the opportunity of chatting with, on my aircraft communication box, during his visit to Nigeria in 1991). A learned friend of mine used to tell me that common law was common sense and that if a man wanted to break a law, he should make sure that it was one commonly broken by commoners. That way, and with luck, my friend reasoned, it might take a long time before the long arm of the law caught up with the law breaker.

London, in 1976, had over three million illegal job seekers, including me. My prayer was that if I was to be caught, it should be after the first three million offenders had been caught. I was convinced that this way I would at least be sure of some respite in the chain of prosecution. For three days I walked the streets of London before I stumbled into the office of an employment agency somewhere around the King's Cross subway station. The agency was just a more refined version of Nigeria's Department for the Unemployed in the Ministry of Labour. The applicants awaiting job placements in the agency cut across different nationalities. The routine was the same: registration was just by writing your name in a register. One major difference, I must mention though, was that the agency was strictly hiring labourers and not skilled hands. This meant that the job seekers got sent to mostly warehouses, or sometimes factories where emergency unskilled labour was required. As a result, I ended up doing all sorts of odd jobs. Well, a job is a job as long as the pay is worthwhile. On the whole, the agency system, from an African's point of view, might be seen as a second enslavement, except that this time it was by choice. The agency paid us our salaries on a weekly basis meaning that being assigned to any job was on a weekly basis. I worked automatically for so many weeks and in many different places such as King's Cross Breweries, Pilkington Glass Factory, an ice cream cold storage and a mattress-foam warehouse. I put in, in the end, twenty weeks of this self-enslavement before I finally ran out of courage. The harsh effects of this slavery in the chilly climate of December 1976 made me pick up my pen and write home for rescue. The rescue letter was six pages long and its contents later turned out to be a weapon that was used against me by my parents whenever I misbehaved after my return to the country. Later, I was to find out that the receipt of the letter in Nigeria brought much welcome joy and relief to my parents. I had left them in total darkness for almost two years as far as my whereabouts was concerned. The little they had known was that I was out of the country, but where exactly I was, they didn't know. My absence had thus continued to cause them gruelling anxiety, until my appeal letter arrived.

I got a reply faster than I had imagined. The letter was brief and straight to the point. I was requested to send a statement of tuition at the flying school which I informed them in my letter that I had been admitted to, and that would be a prelude to their supporting my training.

Going to School

On the 17th of January, 1977, I received a letter from Rogers Aviation International Flight School, Bedford, England, where I had earlier sought for and obtained admission. It was only the non-payment of my tuition fees which had delayed the commencement of my training. The letter now confirmed the payment of my tuition fees, and informed me that the starting date for the course was the 19th of January, 1977. On getting this news, I placed a long distance call to my parents in Nigeria, first to thank them, and secondly to tell them about having received the school's admission letter.

On the morning of the 18th of January, 1977, I caught the intercity British Rail service to Bedfordshire, England. Emerging from the train station in Bedford, I had waiting for me a hand from the school who was there to pick me up for the final phase of my trip to the school. The school's guide at the train station was carrying a shingle with my name written on it in bold letters, and I had a suspicious feeling that he had also been briefed about my being black. Well, if that was truly the case then he was a lucky guy because that morning I was the only black soul that got off the train at Bedford train station. As a matter of fact, I remember the guide just walked towards me and asked politely if I was for Rogers Aviation. It was from him that I learnt that Cranfield Airfield where the school was located was still more than ten miles away from the town of Bedford.

Life in Cranfield village centred upon three major things, namely: the Cranfield Institute of Technology; the Cranfield Airfield where my school was situated; and farmlands. All other activities were just support services to put life in the village in order.

Since my school was a subsidiary of the Cranfield Institute of Technology, I was housed at the Institute's hostel on arrival. Waiting for me in the room were papers welcoming me to the school and providing information about the school and its environment. The most important information to me were instructions about the enrolment process, and that I should report at the school premises the following day. The next day at school, I discovered Rogers Aviation Flight School to be a single building amongst the numerous structures around the airfield. The building had a sign which bore the name of the school, and not very far away was the parking ramp for their trainer aircraft. Entering the building, I was led upstairs where I met the student admissions officer, who put me through the admission formalities.

I was first of all sent to the aviation doctor not far from the school for a fitness check. After being certified fit by the doctor, I was issued a student pilot's certificate with the fitness test forming part of the certificate. This certificate was mandatory before any aspiring flight student could step into an airplane, in keeping with the Civil Aviation Act. As soon as I got back to school from the doctor's, I went through the second formality, which was a flight aptitude test. To do this, I was assigned an instructor specially trained for the purpose. Already, a Cessna 150 trainer aircraft had been prepared for the instructor and me. The instructor walked me towards the ramp where all the school's aircraft were parked, and while we went, he explained strange sounding technical terms to me and how the flight test would be conducted.

As we got to the aircraft, he pointed out the different surfaces of the aircraft, what they were called, and their uses. After talking for thirty minutes, he believed erroneously that I had understood the briefing, and we boarded the aircraft. I now sat in the control cabin of the craft which the instructor had referred to as the "cockpit". I had never been in an aircraft cockpit in my life; this was my first experience. The environment was very much contrary to my imagination. I could only relate to motor cars as the only experience I had in steering. I quickly recognised in front of me what looked the equivalent of a steering wheel in cars, except that it was shaped like a "U" instead of the conventional circular shape of a car steering wheel. On enquiry, the instructor informed me that it was the control stick, but that it could only steer the craft in the air and was almost 96% useless on the ground. Before I could ask how we were going to steer the craft on the ground then, he just pointed to where I was resting my feet. I actually had them on a pair of pedals, because that happened to be the only place I could put them. These pedals steered the aircraft on the ground and were known as rudder pedals. Temporarily ignoring the rest of my cross-examination, the instructor spoke to the control tower, and soon after got the aircraft started up and moving towards the runway. Before I knew what was happening, we were airborne. For some strange reason, I felt very elated during that short transition from ground to air. The flight aptitude test turned out to be a do-as-I-do affair, and after thirty minutes of that we came back down and the instructor pronounced me suitable for the course.

These two admission formalities I had gone through required positive results. It was after the successful completion of both that I was finally issued the school's student identity card. If the case had been otherwise, I would have been rejected by the school and my fees would have been returned in full. I must also point out that the policy of an initial flight aptitude test was unique to Rogers Aviation Flight School. Most other civil aviation flight training schools did not offer aspiring students this opportunity which can easily be seen as an insurance against loss of fees. Some flight schools just took you on, aptitude or no aptitude, as long as you had paid your tuition fees. The longer it took you to go through the course the merrier for such schools, moneywise.

On completion of all pre-admission formalities, I started the ground school phase of my course. In the making of a civil aviation pilot, the training programme is divided into three major courses, each of which attracts an appropriate certificate upon successful completion. The three courses in sequence are (1) the private pilot's course, (2) the commercial pilot's course and (3) the instrument rating/multi-engine aircraft course.

The syllabus of the private pilot's course (PPL) is divided into ground and flight training instructions. The course is tailored in such a way that these training programmes can be simultaneously completed in the shortest possible time. Usually an estimated duration of three months is envisaged in an ideal PPL programme. It is assumed that during this period, you must have gone through four weeks of ground school instruction, and thirty-five hours of flight training. If you are found proficient after the whole programme, you can then go ahead to sit for the Civil Aviation Authority (CAA) ground school examination, and if successful (the CAA pass mark for any examination in flight aviation is 70%) you then get scheduled for the Government Flight Test (GFT). If you are successful here, the authority then issues you a certificate. This is the ideal situation. Over 85% of the time, things never go this way. Take for example my case. I started ground school instruction on the 20th of January, 1977. We were only five students, comprising four males and one female. The female student was British, but had lived in Nigeria when she was young, with her peppermint sweet baron father, Mr Christlieb. There was also a German, one Iraqi, and two of us Nigerians. I spent four weeks in ground school, and passed my CAA examination too. For the flight training, things were not that smooth. The bottom line of the flight training is simply meeting the requirements and achieving the proficiency standards of prescribed CAA manoeuvres. In brief, the CAA requires you to complete a certain number of flight hours under instruction (during the night and day), and having been found proficient by your instructor to fly out alone (that is, going solo, as it is called), the authority requires you to have completed a certain number of hours under this status, both during the day and at night. Having satisfied all these provisos and attained the total minimum of thirty-five hours of flight time with the recommendation from your flight instructor that you are proficient and ready for the government flight test, you then get scheduled for the test that is usually conducted by an external CAA examiner. The rest is good luck and a private pilot's licence if you are successful.

There is a saying in flight schools that "the day you solo is the day you become a pilot". Based on this saying, flight school students have come to be so desirous and proud of the solo tradition. Some coursemates have become sworn enemies just for the trivial reason of one student going solo ahead of a contemporary. The earlier one goes solo, the more clout one wields over the rest of one's class set. The solo record of nine hours in Rogers Aviation was set by a German student some time in the 1960s. I personally do not claim any precocity in the skill of flying. I went solo in the sixteenth hour of flight training, and turned out to be number two in this regard in my set. Incidentally, it was the female student who went solo first. I completed my private pilot's course on the 12th of May, 1977. I achieved this in a total of forty-five hours of flight time. The ironical thing was that I even finished ahead of some students who had gone solo ahead of me. Well, that is what flying, and probably life itself, is all about. Individual progress differs from one person to another. In any form of learning, there are early and late starters alike. For instance, I cannot recall the Indian among us going solo till I left Rogers Aviation, but I recall that he had logged more than eighty-five hours before my departure. The other Nigerian chap had some hard times too. I just didn't see him again after a while.

Acquiring the commercial pilot's licence (CPL) was now the next logical step. Taking the step was quite ideal and in order, but raising the course money was a problem. I had just spent the sum of £3,200 completing the PPL course. Sadly too, Rogers Aviation did not have CAA approval to conduct a CPL course. The only school offering the course in the UK was the Oxford Flight Institute in Oxford, England. Their CPL course fee was a staggering £18,000 for a period of eighteen months. This was the crossroads. For me, that sum of money was just too colossal and obviously unaffordable. I had learnt about the presence of my two elder brothers in the UK by this time too. They were schooling in different polytechnics in London, and I did not need to be told how heavy the financial burden was on my parents. To make matters worse, the amount of money I had spent on my course so far was enough to have almost taken my two brothers together through their entire three-year school programme. And I had expended this amount in less than six months! I considered that this fact alone was enough to extinguish the little spark of enthusiasm that my parents had begun to show. So going to Oxford was clearly a no-dice thing. The solution to this problem, however, came in my securing admission in the USA for the course, and, surprisingly too, at a much lower cost.

In the USA, the course was being offered for $9,000. Thank God it was the peak of the oil boom in Nigeria. The naira was quite strong against the dollar and the tuition fee was to be paid in instalments. The course fee also covered the Instrument and Multi-Engine ratings which meant that all of these courses would now come under one programme. The news of this less expensive bargain was a relief to my now weary parents. The school was Sierra Academy of Aeronautics, Oakland, California.

As soon as I got the first instalment of my tuition fee paid, I didn't waste time in booking a flight for the USA with the legendary, and so far still the air fare discount record holder of the world, Mr Freddie Laker's airline, for the sum of £90, on the 23rd of June, 1977. The magnanimity of Mr Laker was so unique that even for such a low fare, we were still conveyed in the luxury of a DC10 aircraft.

I took ten months to complete my course at Sierra Academy. In that school, I also added a Flight Engineer's Licence to my pilot certificates. I left the USA for Nigeria on the 18th of December, 1978. My mission, which a few years earlier had been just a fantasy, was now fully accomplished.

I arrived in Nigeria in the early hours of 19th December, 1978, fully qualified as a commercial pilot and also as a Flight Engineer (FE). I had in my hand-luggage all my licences. I felt so happy about them that I kept touching them from time to time. At the arrival terminal of the Murtala Muhammed airport (MMA), I had an arrival party made up of my parents and my kid sister waiting for me. My parents were very enthusiastic and transparently happy on seeing me. Unfortunately, I could not reciprocate their feeling as my first sight of them had spoilt my happy mood. I saw standing in front of me a completely white-haired and prematurely aged man. My father had changed so much in two years and my mum standing next to him looked frail too. It made me feel very bad and guilty. It was quite obvious that the strain of working so hard to keep three kids schooling overseas had taken its toll on them. It was a reunion of mixed feelings for me. Till today, I still feel bad any time I recall that scene. We drove back home to Ibadan with me at the wheel. My mother had driven from Ibadan to Lagos because my father's old eye problem had now got worse. No wonder every time he wrote to me the letters were typed. The only giveaway was the not-very-obvious fact that his signatures on these typed letters were not entirely straight on the line. It was obvious that my parents had gone through a lot. Apart from the emotional exchange of greetings, I cannot recall uttering a word for some twenty-five minutes into the journey. The pain and guilt of having put these humble souls through a hardship they never bargained for just kept me tongue-tied.

It appeared as if my mother had read my mind. She broke the ice by telling me in our native Yoruba to make sure I kept the car safely on the road as it was not necessary to get it airborne to prove to them that I could now fly. That was when I realised I had been tearing down the highway. I can also recall her saying that it was okay for me to fly, as long as I was not flying her. That did it. The next thing that came from me was a long verbal diarrhoea of tales and jokes they could never have imagined. The rest of the trip was very interesting with everybody feeling quite happy.

Then came the moment I had been looking forward to: the triumphant presentation of my certificates. We were all seated in the living room, and of course, for the presentation event I was both the actor and the centre of attraction. Incidentally too, I had just arrived from California, where Hollywood is. Meticulously, I picked up my luggage, opened it and brought out a small purse that had in it all my certificates and all the different credit cards I had used when I was in the USA. I opened the purse and brought out my CPL and my FE certificates, both of which I handed over to my father. Then a mild drama ensued. My mother took a look at the certificates and asked my dad in a very sarcastic tone how the credit card-sized paper could be the certificates they had toiled so hard to pay for. As far as she was concerned, it just couldn't be. She turned to me, looking completely disappointed, then she suddenly opened up to my father in our native Ijebu dialect (which I sometimes find a bit difficult to follow), telling him how she had always been sceptical of the whole of my overseas sojourn and how her scepticism had now been justified by some mockery of a paper called a pilot's licence. Well, I can't blame her. She expected to see a larger certificate, the kind common in academic circles. What she didn't know was the simple fact that this certificate was purely a technical document – one that the authorities required the holder to carry at all times when engaged in any flying activity. With the type of certificate she had expected to see, one would need to carry a travelling bag as flight kit any time one went flying. Poor her. She was a trader and had spent a large sum of money training me, so she expected a commensurately large sheet of paper as a certificate. My attorney father was calm about the whole thing.

He had read every detail on that piece of paper and, as far as he was concerned, there was no doubt about the certificate. He just let my mum expend her emotion.

Then he stood up and said in a tone of finality that the answer to my mum's worry was in the job market for pilots. Though the statement was non-committal, it had one strong message: since I had to look for a job very soon, and as long as it was a pilot's job, then I would be presenting these same certificates to the people who, of course, would know the difference. Well, that's the vintage attorney's submission for you. Case closed.

In January 1979 I applied to Nigeria Airways for the post of a pilot. Shortly after, the airline acknowledged receipt of my application and in February I was invited to attend an interview. I was full of excitement on receiving this letter. My goal as a pilot had always been to work for a big air carrier, an airliner with a variety of aircraft to fly. I wanted to be a career airline pilot, and at that time only Nigeria Airways satisfied my desire. So their invitation to an interview was welcome indeed.

It should be recalled that my childhood awe for airplanes led to my dreaming about becoming a pilot. Then the dream was full of nightmares, and as bad as the nightmares were I never woke up. Bravely, I had continued the slumber until that afternoon in February 1979 when I stirred in my dream and woke up only to see my father waving a letter addressed to me from Nigeria Airways. The letter turned out to be the interview invitation, and I found myself fully awake. I woke up to reality now and left my parents to enjoy the freedom and privacy of their thoughts and imagination. I was born and raised in Ibadan and spent some time there before relocating in Lagos, so the news of my presence in town and my new status as a qualified pilot circulated around my circle of friends composed mainly of my colleagues from high school. Having a pilot from their local community was new to most of them, and I enjoyed the glamour of my new status. It was the story of a wonder boy. I was revered by some young lads around my neighbourhood. Some of them even got some admonition from me that has helped them to become pilots today.

The whole scenario was quite interesting. I found out to my surprise that all that my friends knew about aviation came from having been passengers in an aircraft at one time or another. So talking about the making of a pilot was as strange to them as theorising on how the planet earth came to be, or using the voice medium to relate to a deaf person.

Almost There

I left Ibadan on the 14th of February, 1979 to attend the Nigeria Airways interview scheduled for the 16th of that month. In my invitation letter, I had been informed that all necessary arrangements had been made for my smooth passage from Ibadan to Lagos. I was also instructed in the letter to submit the pink form attached to the letter to any Nigeria Airways official on my arrival at Ibadan airport where I would be issued a free ticket for my trip. As I boarded the taxi that conveyed me to the airport in Ibadan on that very hot tropical afternoon, I had so many thoughts rushing through my mind. I couldn't help recalling in my mind the days when I was just that local youth who lived just down the road from the airport who kept wondering every time he saw an aircraft taking off or landing how this feat was made possible. Then it was a big riddle that got me so mesmerised and made me promise myself that, one day, I would solve this riddle, even if it meant becoming part of the riddle itself.

Funnily enough, despite my record-setting experience as an airplane traffic gazer, I had never been to the aerodrome building, even with the advantage of proximity.

Now, alighting from the cab, I walked towards the terminal building, got into the hall and walked to the Nigeria Airways counter. The only counter that was active had a long queue of passengers, all waiting to secure boarding passes. Well, the instruction in my letter was to get in contact with any Nigeria Airways official at the airport. That was the saving grace. The airport had enough Nigeria Airways officials to go round twenty passengers one to one. That made it easy to get in contact with one who was not so busy.

As soon as I made contact, things started happening. The gentleman collected the form I had with me, told me to hold on, and went behind the active checking-in counter. Within a few minutes, he emerged again, but this time with a boarding pass for the flight and the ticket for my return journey. Then the rest of the passengers still waiting in the queue for their boarding passes naturally went irate. Thank God the chap was an old hand in passenger handling. He just grabbed me, shoved me into an office which had the inscription of "Station Manager" on the door, and banged the door shut. I could hear the passengers abusing him and he himself countering in pidgin English that they should hold their peace and if they cared to know, I happened to be one of their pilots. His defence made me stir in my seat. This chap had been very pleasant and helpful, and now he even went as far as awarding me the post of a Nigeria Airways pilot when in reality I was only going to attend the interview. I silently promised to do everything possible to pass the interview, so as not to let down myself and this fellow (whom I had begun to like). Meanwhile, at the counter outside, the passengers' agitation continued to get worse and he too kept revving up to their frequency. At one point I was so sure that at any minute someone was going to slap him. He must be very bold, I surmised. From the little I witnessed in later years, his boldness would have amounted to deliberate suicide.

Eventually, the aircraft landed. The scramble for it then ensued. Little did I know that there was not enough space for everybody. The flight was en route from Benin and the craft already had on board thirty-four passengers out of a total capacity of forty-four people. On the ground in Ibadan, I could count more than forty-nine passengers waiting for this particular flight. I now fully understood what the uproar of the passengers had been all about when I was favoured with a boarding pass. I watched the scramble with keen interest, keeping my cool as instructed by the Nigeria Airways official. He advised me not to worry about the whole scene, and that the captain of the flight was aware of my presence already. He added that if I cared to know, I occupied the category of a must-go passenger. In that case, even if the cabin got filled up, the captain had consented to give me the cockpit's jump seat. I just shook my head in agreement with this guardian angel of mine. What he didn't know, though, was the fact that the seat he said the captain had promised to give out to me might be in the cockpit, but the name he called it was a new one to me. Well, I didn't bother with asking him about that. I left it as an issue between pilots. I eventually got a seat in the cabin, however, and before disembarking the aircraft, my new friend bade me goodbye after advising me to endeavour to say hello to the captain as a matter of courtesy. It was during the exchange of greetings with the captain while airborne that I was shown the jump seat. The jump seat is a seat in an aircraft cockpit usually occupied by an observer pilot. As far as active flying is concerned, it is a redundant seat.

The flight from Ibadan to Lagos was very turbulent though the flight time was under twenty minutes. The turbulence made it seem an eternity. I still recall a high school senior of mine, a doctor by profession, looking over his seat in the cabin towards me, to ask if all was right. Little did he know that neither I nor any pilot for that matter could factually answer that question. Turbulence is one of those odds against the pilot any time he is airborne.

I had no choice but to nod at the doctor with a smile good enough to leave the whole thing to his imagination. He recipro-cated with a look that said, "If it's okay with you, then it's okay with me". I quite admired his attitude in this regard. The rest of the trip was uneventful. To my surprise, while I was deplaning in Lagos, the pair of stewardesses on board the flight wished me good luck in the interview. While I was walking away, I overheard them saying in pidgin English that I was young and lucky. I couldn't help laughing. Young, yes. But lucky? That was a big joke. I had paid my dues to get this far.

I sauntered off with my one-piece hand-luggage to my uncle's home where I had already arranged to spend the next few days. I had another interesting experience during my short stay in my uncle's place. My parents had earlier told these people the purpose of my coming to stay briefly with them. In the evening of the day I arrived there, we had been talking for some time about nothing in particular when it occurred to me that my uncle probably did not believe that I was actually in Lagos to attend a pilot's interview with Nigeria Airways. This was because all through my entire overnight conversation with him, he had questioned me on just about everything involved in being a cabin crew member, but never asked one question about operating as a pilot. At one point I almost lost my cool with him because his disbelief was so transparent any time I tried to remind him that I was in Lagos for a pilot's interview. In the end, I gave up and tried to find a reasonable excuse for his attitude. I just felt that since he was present at my naming ceremony, the picture of me as that infant child was still in his mind, and most of the pilots he must have met so far were hulking guys with enough stamina to lift any aircraft in the Nigeria Airways fleet. If that was the explanation, then it was unfortunate indeed. My uncle, by all standards, was an erudite personality in Nigerian society. At the time I stayed in his house, he had just left his post of Federal Chief Works Officer to head the Nigerian Standards Organisation in Lagos and later on, in Enugu.

It took exactly four years from that night before I finally got my uncle's scepticism about my professional status permanently interned. It all happened on the 28th of August, 1983, during one of my flights from Enugu. Then I was a substantive first officer on the B737 aircraft. We had just flown into Enugu from Lagos and I was with one of my few revered captains, Captain Oyedeji. We had just finished disembarking the passengers we brought from Lagos when the captain ordered the boarding of Lagos-bound passengers from Enugu. As was usual with young bachelors bustling with energy, I was gazing hawk-like at the embarking queue of passengers for Lagos with the hope of making contact with a damsel or two if any, when I suddenly spotted my Doubting Thomas uncle in the queue. Wow! Was I happy! This was the moment of truth, and this was my long and painfully awaited time to pay back. I calmed down my excitement because I really planned to enjoy this unexpected break to the fullest. Before I put my plan into action, I told my captain what it was all about.

I summoned the head of the cabin staff with us that morning, and I pointed to my uncle, who was in the queue, almost near the step of the aircraft and about to ascend it, and instructed the crew member to summon my uncle to the cockpit in a tone of an official directive that must make it clear and urgent as if a standing order from the captain. I clearly instructed him that under no condition should he reveal my presence in the cockpit. The crew must have conveyed the message perfectly because no sooner had my uncle entered the aircraft than he just walked as fast as he could to the cockpit, carrying the look of a crew-persecuted passenger hoping to find cover under the captain.

As soon as he entered the cockpit, he announced his presence in a polite and respectful manner to the captain. Captain Oyedeji, in his vintage humorous way, responded first by asking my uncle to have a seat, then he melodramatically thumbed the electrical lock switch for the cockpit door and locked it. He then started his speech, directed at my uncle: "Sir, you are welcome to this cockpit. My name is Oyedeji and I happen to be the captain of this flight. My presence here is no coincidence; it has been a long and tiring design in tracking you down. I would like to inform you that I represent the illegal and unregistered union of the Non-standard Organisation of Nigeria, with her mobile head-quarters in Alaba Market, Mile 2, Lagos. I am under strict instruction from my fellow union members, who are awaiting the arrival of this flight in Lagos, to make sure I never let you out of my sight, because they need to discuss with you the colossal amount of money they have lost because of your alarmingly effective standard control of their vastly defective goods." The captain now turned to me and said in Yoruba that I should keep the gentleman under strict surveillance all the way to Lagos. It was only then that I turned around, to look at my uncle for the first time, and burst out laughing. "Good afternoon and welcome aboard once again," I said.

He looked at me for a while, before he said, "Taiwo, what you guys have done to me is not good at all. I almost had a heart attack. Thank God it was only a practical joke. Anyway, how are you, and why haven't you come to visit all these days?" As part of the plan, I did the flying to Lagos, and when we arrived, I rounded off the trip with a beautiful landing. Before my uncle disembarked, he thanked the captain and me for giving him the rare but initially scary opportunity in an aircraft cockpit for the first time, and then he bade us goodbye. As I found out months later, he went to tell our extended family this story.

In the morning of the 16th of February, 1979, I had left my uncle's house for the interview venue. That morning, I had on the best of my suit and tie collection from England. In my opinion, I was looking my best that morning. The only sad thing was that although since my arrival in my uncle's house he had been so nice in ensuring that one of his cars was always at my disposal, on the day of my interview none was provided me. And this was simply because my uncle disliked the idea of a relation of his taking up a job that entailed serving people in public. (He still believed I was attending the interview for the post of an airline flight attendant.) Denying me the use of his car was, therefore, a way of registering his disapproval. In my suit and tie, I self-consciously caught a danfo minibus as early as 6.30 that morning from my uncle's Abule-Oja area of Lagos, hoping to arrive in Ikeja after numerous bus connections.

Inside the bus, I discovered that I wasn't the only suit-and-tie passenger on board, and this made me feel less piqued about having to take that mode of transportation on what I considered to be one of the most important days in my life. Discovering that what I had considered my pitiable situation was just a normal way of life for other people was also a big solace. I noticed, however, that all the other guys in suits were carrying a pair of handkerchiefs each, and it wasn't long before I realised why. These guys sure were experienced bus passengers: we were all sweating like pigs, but they just dried their sweat gracefully with their handkerchiefs. I had learnt a big lesson here.

The rest of the trip was full of the mundane incidents that characterised Lagos community. If it was not a traffic jam, then it was an accident or even a house on fire on the roadside. God, what an interesting trip that was! I had a bus change at Oshodi bus stop, and this time, it was the bigger and usually more congested molue bus. I wished the ride in it could have taken longer. It was such great fun. One comedy I recall vividly involved a chap who had boarded the bus shortly after I did, carrying a big bag. No sooner was he aboard the vehicle than he began in a baritone voice to advertise traditional medical herbs for all ailments imaginable. What tickled me was when he changed gear to advertise his performance-enhancing herbs for sexual intercourse and other activities. The climax came while he was explaining to a seemingly interested passenger some herbal prescription for eye problems. He just left all passengers aboard gasping for breath when he offered as a bonus to the passenger, another herb that would make him have another eye at the back of his head: "My brother, I dash you this strong one. E go make you get eye for back." I got to my destination and it was time to get off the bus. I alighted at the airport First Bank bus stop after a mild drama with the bus conductor who pretended he had forgotten that I had some change to collect from him.

At the bus stop, I inquired about the direction to Nigeria Airways House, the indicated interview venue. From the directions I got at the bus stop it was easy to locate the place. After a seven-minute walk, I sighted ahead of me the neon inscription in big letters: "NIG★RIA A★RW★YS HOUSE", and although some letters were missing, the meaning was quite clear. Already I could see the flow of human traffic around the building. As soon as I entered the premises, my mind went back to the interview scene at the Federal Ministry of Forestry. This time, it wasn't a festival but clearly one of these free concerts at the New York Central Park, the only missing thing being the music. It was the American accent and colloquialism all the way. People gathered in different factions, and all you had to do was choose the bunch that you would easily fit into. The choice was determined by certain provisos. In my case, the guys I joined had trained in American flight schools. Some were, indeed, my colleagues at my own flight school. I also identified some personality preferences in the group. This way one was assured of a pleasurable waste of time conversing with other members of the group while waiting for the interview to commence.

I had arrived at the venue at exactly 7.05 a.m., fifty-five minutes before the slated time of 8.00 a.m. At exactly 8.00 a.m., a Nigeria Airways official came out from one of the offices in the building and announced that the interview would commence at 10.00 a.m., instead of the 8.00 a.m. indicated in the invitation letters. He then went on to distribute some forms for us to fill in with some relevant information about ourselves. I soon completed mine and submitted it. I was later to realise that the order of the interview was based on the order of submission of the forms, and my number was 103! However, by 3.00 p.m., it was my turn to be interviewed. Many other applicants had not been so lucky and had to return the following day for their own interview.

Before I go on to talk about the interview, I would like to mention a certain fellow (my interview hero, so to speak) who, in spite of all the stampede around the venue, stood out clearly from the whole crowd. What first caught my attention were his clothes. He was fully dressed in a pilot's uniform, from the cap to his shoes. He was impeccably clean, and I was further awed when I saw that he had three epaulette lines sewn onto both shoulders. As a pilot, that was the rank of a Senior First Officer (SF/O). With that status, the chap was just overqualified for the job I was also seeking. I hoped and prayed that Nigeria Airways was in need of more than just one pilot; if not then I should just start heading back home. I knew well enough that an SF/O holds an Airline Transport License (ATPL), and also a total flying experience of over 1,500 hours. With all these, he is qualified for any pilot's position all over the world. And there was I with barely 230 hours, competing with this chap for a job. It turned out, however, that the airline did need more than one pilot, and I thanked God for that. At exactly 3.00 p.m., the voice of Nigeria Airways (as we quickly named the chap calling out the numbers) came out and bellowed, "Number 103." Hearing this, I picked up the file containing all my documents, and walked towards the interview office, wondering how many applicants in the calibre of my SF/O hero were left in the crowd.

The Interview

The interview panel consisted of eight people seated and looking very eager to do their job. The most distinguished member of the panel was a gentleman, seated in the middle of the other members of the panel. He was a fine-looking man and turned out to be head of the panel.

Before I could even utter a word, he smiled at me and said, "Good afternoon, young man, I am Captain Billy Eko." He glanced at the form on the table in front of him, and said, "You must be Mr Fatungase."

"Yes, sir," I acknowledged cautiously. He then offered me a seat and advised me to relax as much as I could. Then my tie appeared to have caught his attention and he remarked that he liked it. That remark just got me relaxed. As far as I was concerned, the head of the panel seemed a reasonable gentleman. So, at least, if anything went wrong in the process of being interrogated by the rest of the panel members this man would be more than capable of setting things right. He then requested both the original and photocopies of all the documents I claimed in my CV. As soon as I handed them over to him, he passed the documents to the officer seated next to him. What followed was juror-like. The documents were passed around all the members, and after conferring in low tones for a few minutes with the members, Captain Eko looked up at me, asked me some questions and announced to me that if I was successful in the interview, I should prepare my mind to attend an assessment course at the Zaria Flight Institute before I could be fully integrated into Nigeria Airways. He also advised me to have my American Commercial Pilot's Licence (CPL) certificate converted to the Nigerian equivalent. That was all, and he bade me a good afternoon. I left the office with a ray of hope of being employed. Also, I now had to find out the procedure for converting my licence to the Nigerian equivalent as advised by the panel head.

The Licence Conversion Debacle

The issuance and conversion of any civil aviation certificate in any country is the sole responsibility of that country's civil aviation governing authority. Therefore, my next assignment was going to the Nigerian Federal Ministry of Civil Aviation with the hope of achieving the conversion. I never gave converting my licence any serious thought because I had already gone through this process in the USA, when I had to convert the UK Private Pilot's Licence in my possession to the American one, before I could be permitted by law to commence the next phase of my training (the CPL programme). The conversion involved filling in appropriate forms for the licence I was applying for. I was issued the licence the next day.

Sadly, this was not to be the case in my encounter with the Nigerian Civil Aviation officials. Although I had the opportunity of serving in a government ministry before, I was completely oblivious of the red tape in government business perhaps because of my status as a junior civil servant then. At the Ministry of Civil Aviation, I tasted for the first time the sweet and sour menu of government bureaucracy. The first time I went to the ministry to inquire about the conversion it was a day of tales of fear. I was told by an official that I would have to write exams in aircraft loading, and that after passing that, I would have to see a Mr Macaulay who would then schedule me for another examination called "air law". Then the official went into the rhetoric of how difficult it was to pass these exams, and how so many pilots trained in the USA had had to repeat these exams several times. He then ended his sermon of discouragement by warning me about the person of Mr Macaulay. The gentleman wielded autocratic powers in licence issuance and might be very irascible if I happened to be dealing with him on his bad day. I thanked the official very much for demonstrating consummate skills in the devolution of information, and asked him (since he seemed so well-informed in the area of licensing) where I could get the textbooks that I required to get ready for these examinations. But he informed me sadly in pidgin English that the problem of the exams lay in the shameful fact that the books I needed for them were as scarce as chicken in Ethiopia. "But I may look around to get them for you," he said. "Only it's going to cost you some investment."

For me, as long as he got the books, I was ready to reward him. The most ridiculous part of all this was that the ministry was the only supplier of these books, yet but by error or design they did not seem to have had any in their library for over a decade, and nobody seemed to be raising any alarm about it. Anyway, I got the books, and studied them. For the loading exam, I had to employ the services of an instructor who was also recommended from the ministry. The whole exam resembled a syndicated operation.

After the instructor was satisfied with my performance and progress, he advised me to book an appointment for the exams. It was while doing this that I met the much-talked-about Mr Macaulay. That morning, as I got to the premises of the ministry, I looked for my ministry pal and informed him that I was ready to see Mr Macaulay. He conducted me to the front of an office that had Mr Macaulay's name inscribed on it and wished me good luck. I knocked at the door cautiously and a very normal voice invited me to come inside. I opened the door and entered Mr Macaulay's office. The man himself didn't look up for a while and didn't say anything either. He had his head down with a pen in his hand and was busy writing. On his desk, he had such a mountain of files and documents that one could never have eye contact with him unless he looked up from them. Well, immediately he looked up, I prostrated myself and greeted him in the English language. Obviously amused by this, he demanded officiously what mission had brought me to his office. After I narrated my mission, he requested to see my American licence and my log book. (The log book is a booklet where pilots record their flying experience in the form of hours and minutes.)

He looked through these documents meticulously and then gave me an application form to fill in for the licence conversion. He then scheduled me for the exams. To my surprise, as I was about to leave his office, he called me back, brought out a copy of the supposedly scarce air law textbook and for the next twenty-five minutes or so, pointed out to me the areas of importance in the book as far as the test was concerned. He then said goodbye. God! I had heard so many things about this middle-aged frail-looking man and I expected to meet a sadist. What a life and what a bunch of treacherous characters he had around him, pilots and ministry officials alike! I learnt a great lesson in life there, which is that most people in this world only use language to either conceal their real thoughts or confuse the other party.

In the end, I sat for these exams, and contrary to the adverse information about repetition of these exams, I passed both at the first attempt. This made me form the opinion that the ministry officials (the unscrupulous ones) used the act of intimidation to steal from the pockets of their usually ignorant victims, mostly from the USA. I was subsequently issued the Nigerian CPL.

With this in my possession, the ground had now been cleared and ploughed, but the harvest was still being awaited (that is, the interview result). While waiting at home, I prayed hard every day for a positive outcome. God, the Lord of harvests, finally answered my prayers. In the afternoon of the 23rd of March, 1979, my father had another letter for me, again from Nigeria Airways, which turned out to be an offer of employment for the post of an Operation Assistant on Grade Level 06, and an annual salary of N1,944:00k.

Now, trouble once more: first, the letter did not indicate anything about this position being a temporary one pending final assessment at the aviation institute in Zaria. Then, there was nothing on that paper that said I was a pilot, not to speak of being employed as one. My father read the letter, took one look at me and went straight for the telephone in the living room, and dialled my mum's shop. The message to her was very short: start heading home. As soon as my mum arrived, he just told her to pack a few things and that we were going to Lagos. Before my mother could say a word, he dangled the letter in front of her and said, "Just let us go. Before the end of today, we shall know who your son is. Right here, I have a letter that at least we can use to solve this riddle." A few minutes after that, they left.

They came back to Ibadan at about 9.00 p.m. that night. They tried to say "hello" to me but I just walked away from them. I had concluded that they had gone to the airways and done their investigation and that, of course, it had all come to nothing. Then, the following day, I had just finished dressing and was on my way out when my mother, putting on her best smile, said to me, "Mr Pilot, aren't you going to have a meal before you go out?" I just smiled and walked away. As far as I was concerned, it was my turn to get funny too and I was sure going to enjoy myself. Their conduct towards me all along had made me feel like the modern-day "419 Fraud" accused, although their reaction was only normal and fair since they were my parents and sponsors. They helped in confirming the belief I had formed about the word "fair" being a cosmetic one. Why? If this world were fair, as I had always argued with my attorney father, there would be no need for a Ministry of Justice, and, of course, attorneys too. So someone like my father would either not have a job, or would have been in some other profession. There was a truce in the end; I had learnt a long time earlier that it was a no-win situation feuding with one's parents.

At last, I assumed duty officially with Nigeria Airways on the 26th of March, 1979. Remember, during my interview the panel had given me an insight into the company's policy regarding new pilot intakes trained in the USA. I had been informed that we would be required to attend an assessment course at the Institute of Civil Aviation Flight Training School in Zaria. I still could not comprehend the rationale behind this policy. As far as I was concerned, I had a qualified pilot certificate already and I just couldn't see what we were going to be taught in that school that would complement the licence I had trained hard to obtain. I have under the subheading, "The Story in a Blitz", expressed in a summarised form the events that happened, before I finally got trained on the F27 aircraft by Captain Ogunaike.

The first shock I had on assumption of duty with Nigeria Airways was the revelation that out of the large number of applicants that had gathered on my interview day, only nine of us had come out successful. And it was no surprise at all when I found that my interview hero was one of the nine. As Operation Assistants (the status we were offered) we were sent to the flight operation dispatch office to assume duty. The dispatchers (unknown to us) had been eagerly awaiting with two sets like ours previously, so they already had a tradition of how to handle us. Ours was quite an odd situation. In an airline environment, the dispatcher is ostensibly a subordinate or, better still, the principal assistant to the pilot on the ground. Later on in this book, I shall explicitly delineate the role this group of people play in flight execution. So one could easily anticipate the type of work climate this odd set-up would eventually lead to. The bottom line is that it led to acrimony between members of the two groups. The day we assumed duty, we reported to one Mr Nkadi, who I must say was a down-to-earth and intelligent chap. He was the assistant head of the office. The only thing he told us was a matter-of-fact thing. He just said, "Gentlemen, there's really nothing for you guys here as far as the office goes, but since the airline has adopted this fantastic policy for reasons best known to it, please just do me the favour of putting in an appearance at this office every day and there will be no problem." Later on, we (my group) were to meet the overall head of the office, who turned out to be a pain in the neck. He did his best to boss us around, but failed woefully for the simple reason that he needed reinforced effort, since he could hardly locate us most times. If I had liked him, I would have referred him to that omnipotent peddler in the molue bus to kindly sell him the herb that sprouted another eye at the back of his head. That way, he would at least possess a wider field of vision to help him in his efforts to locate us.

Before we knew it, we had already spent one month in this office, and suddenly it was our first pay-day. God, what a day, and what an event! We didn't know that, as junior staff, we would be receiving our pay in envelopes. Apart from this, we had to queue up. The first time we were dumbfounded about the whole thing. I was so stupid that I took my place in the queue behind a line of more than two hundred people. We were really queuing for the dole, and it sure was a big pain in the arse. One major experience was the animosity from different working units of the airline towards the pilot fold. It was common to hear someone in the crowd on pay day pass opprobrious remarks like: "Aha! So pilots too come here to queue for money!" The annoying thing was the fact that we were not the first set of pilots, so why continue the fuss. The reason can only be one thing: some form of complex.

The aspersion got worse for us as time went on. But thank God, it ended after six cruel months. In September 1979, we got a memo informing us to proceed to Zaria for the assessment course. God, what a relief! But before the narrative changes scene, let me dwell a little longer on this matter of aspersion by some groups within the airline against pilots and flight engineers in the company. This manifested itself, once again, on the wet evening of the 18th of July, 1983, while I was operating as a first officer under the command of one of my mentors, Captain Okiwelu, on service WT 112, scheduled for Port Harcourt and with a return and final leg to Lagos. It was one of those flights we refer to as night-owl flights (the aircraft was a B737, registration 5N-ANW).

That night, with the odds against us, what with the night itself and the thunderstorms, Captain Okiwelu was still his magnanimous and pleasant self and allowed me to fly the aircraft into Port Harcourt Airport. He even showed that his magnanimity cut across boundaries by allowing the then station accountant for Nigeria Airways in Port Harcourt to take a seat in the cockpit with us since the passenger cabin was already full. I recall that I tried to dissuade the captain from admitting this man into the cockpit because of his (the accountant's) perpetual reluctance to pay bona fide crew allowance. As a matter of fact, it was customary for this fellow to come close to engaging in a brawl before paying employees money they were legally entitled to. In spite of all this, the captain still obliged him the cockpit seat.

The night was cloudy and wet. Even at Lagos, the departure field was shrouded in rain showers too. Well, unfortunately for the accountant, it was his first time in an aircraft cockpit. What a misfortune for him, because even during daytime non-crew members still feel uncomfortable sitting in the cockpit, not to speak of night-time. I will say it any day that for an untrained hand to ride in the cockpit at night is a bizarre experience. In the cockpit at night, apart from the silhouettes of the crew, the rest is a circus of lights here and there, coupled with a series of incomprehensible (to a layman) radio transmissions from different aircraft stations to the air traffic control unit. Then in our own case, since it was a cloudy night, the aircraft was engulfed in cloud as well, so that visibility beyond the aircraft window was definitely out of the question. For a layman, this is where to pray hard that the pilots flying you actually know what they are doing. To make matters worse for our station accountant, I was the one doing the flying with all these bizarre things (in his thinking) going on. I knew, for sure, that he was utterly confounded because from the time we took off till the time we landed in Port Harcourt in heavy rain showers, he never, at any time, uttered a word. I must say though, that while we were still in cruise, I really enjoyed this chap's presence in the cockpit because I could not bring myself to believe that the hulking bully could wear such a grim look and breathe so quickly and audibly that I could not help winking at the captain and nudging him to take a look at the poor guy. I even

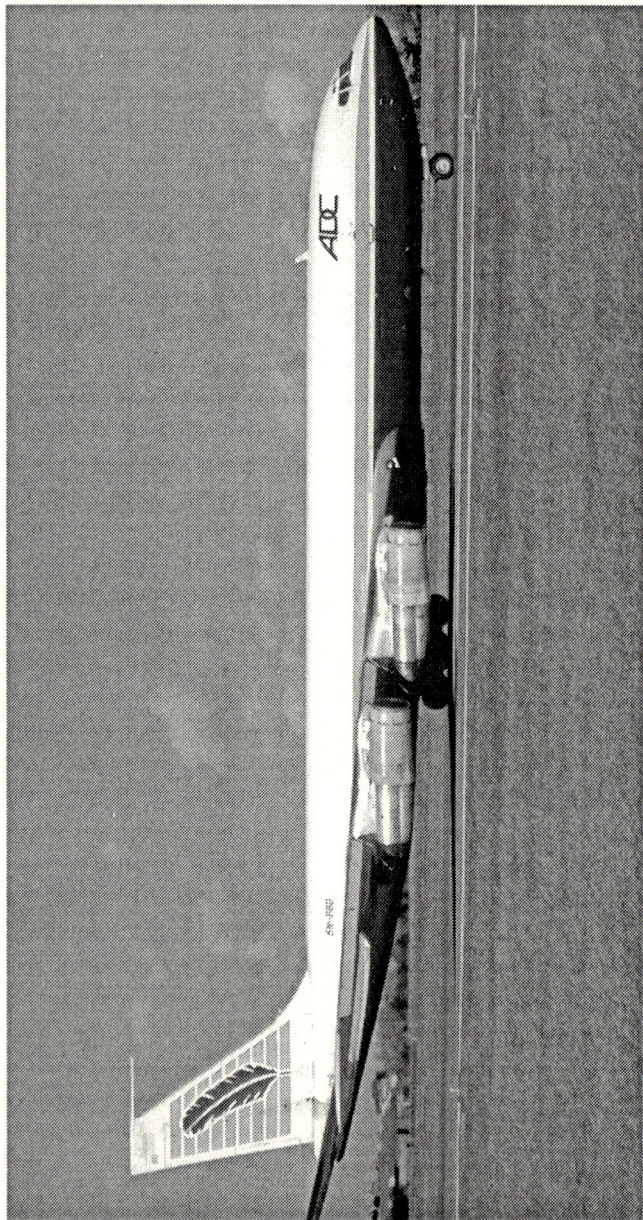

Boeing 707 Airplane. Courtesy: ADC Airline

cracked a joke through the cockpit intercom system (so that the chap wouldn't hear), that the guy was about to have a heart attack any moment if we didn't get our arses down in Port Harcourt as soon as possible. I was not far from the truth. As soon as we parked the aircraft, the fellow just burst into relieved chatter. He remarked breathlessly: "God, captain, I didn't see a thing. This co-pilot of yours is a captain, too. I don't know how to thank you guys. But one thing I have learnt tonight, this job of yours is not easy at all. As for me, I will never again in my life delay the payment of any crew allowance."

Then still in a trance, he asked the captain if he could pay us one night-allowance each. Then the vintage Okiwelu I knew, seized the opportunity to educate the guy and politely turned down the illegal payment. Immediately, he concluded his self-confession; it was now clear to me that this man's habit of giving flight crews a headache regarding payment of allowances had been a deliberate and callous act all along. I must emphasise here however, that this custom was not peculiar to this accountant. There were numerous Nigeria Airways station accountants guilty of this rather sordid behaviour in the line of duty.

The Zaria Experience and the Making of a Productive Second Officer

Before I start to narrate the Zaria experience, I would like to reiterate here that, even till today, my recalcitrant stance in this area of the company's policy would always remain the same. The company's sending already qualified pilots for assessment in Zaria, especially the ones from the USA, is nothing but an acrimonious policy. So many qualified US-trained pilots are today flying in different airlines and in large numbers as captains and co-pilots alike, and are performing quite well too, to say the least. I do not know of any local competitor of Nigeria Airways that has this rather regressive policy of sending qualified pilots for more training. Pilots trained in the USA form the major cockpit composition of these airlines. Also, so far these airlines can boast of a relatively accident-free record.

Well, my set of March 1979 had the names of nine individuals. (1) O O Bankole, (2) John O Agboso, (3) J I Ahuche, (4) I Ikpeme, (5) D Charles, (6) T Fatungase, (7) F Nwagbo, (8) F Owagbemi, (9) O O Bonojo. Our set was called the MTP 8 set. As far as getting a final divorce from redundancy was concerned, going to Zaria was a much welcome development. At least there would be a temporary change of scene. And although I saw whatever we were going to be taught in Zaria as an unnecessary repetition of our earlier flight training, at least we would be engaged in the aviation field one way or another. That in itself was a big relief for me.

It was when we were about to leave for Zaria that I collected my first Duty Travel Allowances of N514:00k from the company to cover my stay of six weeks in Zaria. Smiling contentedly with our allowances in our pockets, my colleagues and I departed Lagos on the 23rd of September, 1979, on a Nigeria Airways F28 night coach service to Kaduna. The captain of the flight, Captain

Ikomi (who now has a Ph.D. in some academic discipline), gave us a very smooth flight. After about an hour's cruise, we arrived at the old Kaduna Airport. The Nigeria Airways station manager in Kaduna was already waiting for us, with chartered taxis to take us to Zaria. It was my first time at Kaduna Airport, and it was dark. I would have loved to see the airport in daylight.

The trip to Zaria was a scary one. Unfortunately, I was in one of those "land jet" cars, so it was jet speed all the way. Thank God the driver knew the road quite well, otherwise it would have been a disastrous trip. In spite of all, we got to Zaria in one piece. Unfortunately, we arrived quite late at about 11.00 p.m. local time. The school's reception party had got tired of waiting for us and had left. Realising this, we had no choice but to look for hotel accommodation. We got one close to the Institute. It was the Zaria Hotel. While we were going through the checking-in formality at the hotel, we came to realise that the hotel staff knew our mission in the town and were even later on to relate interesting events that happened to the two sets that had been before us. The hotel staff were so informed that they gave us information which we found out later on to be very accurate, regarding our instructors (both ground and flight), who wasted no time showing their prejudice against American-trained pilots found wanting, by subjecting them to demeaning conditions. This in turn, led the American-trained pilots to display some aversion to the instructors. This tradition of mutual aversion continues year after year. The hotel staff concluded in their quite generous and fair admonition that humility from each American-trained pilot would be helpful in reducing the misunderstanding between the two parties.

We spent only a night at the Zaria Hotel. The following morning, we were at the premises of the Institute. We appeared with our luggage in their office premises to officially report our arrival. The school officials were quick to react to our presence. From the office premises, we were immediately taken to the school's housing grounds and allocated to different rooms. Since the rooms were very spacious, we decided among ourselves to occupy them in pairs. Actually the building was a big two-storey block built as a hostel for the school's female students. Judging from the size of that building, it was apparent that the school had expected a high female intake, which had not been so. The building was indeed very large. At the time we were there, the school could only boast of two female students, and until we left the school, that number did not increase. My room-mate was Mr Jerry Ahuche (now a captain). He was older than me and this natural inequality turned out to be a source of harmony between us. His maturity clearly oiled the nexus of our relationship in living together and this also put and end to all forms of animosity that usually occur between people of different cultural back-grounds. He was an intelligent extrovert and a convivialist of great principle. Overall, we shared a few opinions together and were able to go through the programme together with little pain.

We started our course two days after our arrival. We were to find out that the syllabus was more or less a facsimile of the American Commercial Pilot's License (CPL) syllabus. The only difference was that in Zaria we delved into full details of all the subject matters. In the USA, this was not the case in most flying schools. Subject details in the USA were tailored towards the subject tests. Any other information outside the scope of the test paper format was considered irrelevant.

Trying to teach all these topics in full detail, would have taken the same duration or more, that one spent going through it in the flying school. In cognisance of this, the whole course had to be compressed (the ground school), and in effect the information was put in shorthand form. This led to the use of loaded words that carried vast information in them. The course duration target was forty days and knowing this, one did not need to be told that only hard work coupled with full directional interest in the course was the insurance against failing.

I must say that the Institute of Civil Aviation, Zaria, like any other higher institution of learning, was designed to create serenity, stamping firmly in one's mind an environment of learning. Adequate provisions were made for the different needs of all the people dwelling in that community. Facilities ranging from learning to recreational, including entertainment, were provided. Things were made so easy that, as a student, all one had to contribute towards success was simply meaningful school attendance. With this and with luck on one's side, success should come at the end as a routine thing. The smooth intercourse between the school's ground and flight training was a unique one worthy of emulation by other flight schools. I later discovered that both the ground and flight instructors had worked so hard to achieve a hand-in-glove working relationship. This I am sure, was the magic (or trade secret) behind the school's flight training integration success. The school owned adequate training facilities for all facets of civil aviation training, i.e. aircraft maintenance engineering, air traffic control and radio technology.

Well, we came for a specially outlined programme tailored to meet our company's needs. We took classes in subjects such as Flight Planning, Weather, Instrument, Aerodynamics of Flight and a few other not-so-familiar subjects such as Radio Aids, Performance A and Navigation General. Different ground instructors took us in these subjects. I must say that all the instructors clearly demonstrated consummate understanding of their subjects. It was sincerely a case of back to school days. Their unique teaching methodology made the assimilation of the topics relatively easy for an average student. Despite my initial scepticism, I must confess that I really enjoyed the programme. There were two characters among the ground instructors that I would always remember for their exceptionally articulate communication skills, their down-to-earth ways and who-gives-a-damn-about-who-you-are-or-where-you-come-from attitude.

One of these personally revered instructors of mine took us in the weather subject while the other took us in the rather confusing and anachronistic subject called Navigation General. The former just couldn't get over the fact that we were going to become high income earners (so to speak) as soon as we got back to work, and that he who supposedly made us would still remain on his same salary grade level. I just couldn't catch his drift because I did not see what his pay had to do with pilots. We had to help him bury his gripe by referring him to the arbitration panel on salaries at the Federal Ministry of Labour. One of my colleagues even referred him to his highly placed uncle at the ministry. This instructor later got so pedantic that the only thing missing in his pedantry was the omission of his name from the textbook we used for his class. He also turned out to be one of those the Zaria Hotel staff had given us hints to watch out for. He was quite a worldly and civilised personality, which made him carry this macho image around himself. We were able to gather that he had been in the school for over a decade. This gave him the élan of the man to worship, and brings me to the issue of student/instructor relationships in that school. It was just a plain master and servant thing. But here, we didn't have much problem in making it clear to the instructors that we were qualified hands and not students.

We spent a period of three weeks in the ground school, and then wrote exams on the subjects we had been taught. The tests were not easy, especially the one on that humble subject called Navigation General. From the results in that subject alone, one could see that navigation was not general at all. Though I remember scoring highest in the subject, I detested it so much that I didn't even feel any joy or relief about having passed it. A couple of guys had to resit the examination. The annoying thing was knowing all along that this particular subject was a complete waste of precious time. To date, I still have not found any use for all the information gathered in that subject because even before we left for Zaria, it was common knowledge that the advanced navigational technology already incorporated into almost all aircraft flying then and today had rendered the whole idea behind that subject obsolete. At the end of ground instruction, I came out second overall in my set, with 84% aggregate. And leaving this behind us, we went on to face the almighty flight instructors.

Our encounter with the flight instructors can simply be defined as the petty contest of status hegemony. As far as that was concerned, it was a classic case of abuse of the culture of sociometrics. No matter how one tried, it was just a complete mess.

These guys had already made up their minds about us. Luckily for both parties, word was sent from Lagos for the termination of all flight assessments. So, the only contact we had with these people ended in the school's flight simulation trainer known as the Link (named after the inventor Mr Ed Link).

Talking about flight simulation, the Link equipment itself is the most primary form. It is a simulated aircraft cockpit, without the fuselage. ("Fuselage" is a French word which refers to the aircraft body structure.) This simulated cockpit is complete with all the seats in it and aircraft instrumentation. It also incorporates the latest electrical and computer technology to produce the sense of sound and motion, plus other conditions that would activate all mediums of perception in a crew. After achieving this, flight crews can now practise in this dummy box, with a trained hand called an instructor who introduces, in hypothetical forms, the manoeuvres that can be achieved in a real airplane and more, at the same time bypassing real life situations like the presence of passengers and the risk of death resulting from certain manoeuvres or false moves that may sometimes lead to a crash. As a matter of fact, this fantastic technological breakthrough known as the flight simulator is the bottom line of flight training.

We did flight simulation for about one and a half weeks with the instructors in Zaria before we finally left for Lagos. Arriving in Lagos, we were upgraded from our junior status as operation assistants to the senior status of second officers. From now till we left the employment of Nigerian Airways, we would continue to maintain our commensurate status as pilots.

It was a long and unpleasant journey to career flying due to lack of planning coupled with organised disorganisation which itself was a product of haphazard policy formation and implementation. This was further confirmed in the process of being issued complete pilots' uniforms. So much importance was attached to crew uniform that I was given some sort of paper authorising British Airways properties section to provide me with all necessary flight crew uniform items needed. Suffice it to say that I ended up travelling to London to collect these items. The moment I collected them, I knew straight away that the real task had finally started. I was to realise later on in my career that the glamour and the risks of the job were interwoven. My personal belief after realising this was that *flying* and *dying* sounded very much alike and were easily interchangeable. All one had to do was delete the first two letters from the word "flying" and substitute the letter "D" and the resulting word would of course be "dying". Well, so much for that.

The next event and happily the final one, before we were handed over to Captain Ogunaike, started with a memo on the

27th of December, 1979: fifteen others and me to attend the F27 conversion course. This was strictly in consonance with civil aviation laws which stipulate that for any aircraft to be flown by any crew, each crew member must have successfully undergone ground and flight training courses prescribed for the particular aircraft to be flown and obtained a certificate of authorisation from the governing Civil Aviation Authority (CAA). This certificate, which comes in the form of a stamp in the crew member's licence, is what is generally referred to in aviation parlance as the "aircraft type rating". Without this, it is illegal to operate as a crew member on any aircraft.

The Ground School

We attended the F27 ground school in the only training facility (then) of the company, known as the Manpower Building. The course was conducted in one of the rooms in the old and faded one-storey structure that housed cat-sized rats as permanent tenants. It was a far cry from the learning environment in Zaria. A few metres away from the building was the only road leading to the local wing of the Murtala Mohammed Airport, which housed the local wing of the Nigeria Airways terminal building. The location of this building made the everyday blast of car horns a major part of the whole course.

The course was only for four weeks, but turned out to be quite unpleasant, to say the least. The first shock I got from the school was the fact that while my set was in Zaria wading through all the academic and physiological problems, the company had conducted an interview for more pilots and employed them. More shocking was the fact that these new intakes had been given senior staff positions as second officers (which of course, made them our seniors) and had even been trained on the F27 aircraft before our arrival. This, of course, made me feel immediately as if I had just arrived from a labour camp. And although the policy of having American-trained pilots assessed in Zaria was finally revoked, this had cost my set its proper position of seniority.

Life went on, however. Ground school was under way and we were lectured on the different systems of the F27 aircraft. All in all, three ground school instructors shared the systems syllabus. They turned out to be expert hands in the respective systems syllabus they each taught. The gentlemen were very pleasant guys too. Apart from the sometimes not-too-conducive lecture environment provided by the airline, one remarkable aspect of the protocol was the graceful hospitality of the company in making sure that our stay in class every day was worthwhile, apart from the blaring of car horns, that is. Provision was made to feed us on palatable dishes. The class itself was made almost soundproof. One other problem which was never solved however, was the landlord's: the rats.

At the end of the course, we took a mock test, specially tailored towards the ministry's examination. A few days later, we were scheduled for the real examination. The outcome of that examination was a record disaster. Sixteen of us had sat for this examination, and only one made it, and with a borderline pass too. The cut-off point in any aviation test is 70%. Our lucky chap scored 71%. God, what an outcome!

We all learnt one vital lesson from this, though. Apart from the ministry admitting to having given us an examination meant for ground engineers, which of course, from a pilot's point of view, was too technical, our real undoing was ignorance of the newly adopted scoring pattern of the ministry, which was to deduct a certain mark for any questions failed. Thus, if you were not sure of the right answer to a question, the standard procedure was to entirely abstain from answering it, in order not to lose marks already earned from other correct answers. Armed with this knowledge, we all passed the test the second time around.

The last test was the performance examination which formed an integral part of the aircraft course itself. This course by law entailed mastery of the aircraft behaviour under certain conditions; its gross take-off weight and her landing weight under sub-conditions like outside temperature, outside pressure altitude, runway length, and so on. The examination involved basically the reading and plotting of graphs as accurately as possible. It was after passing this test that I finally met Captain Ogunaike.

Flying the F27

Luckily, things got into shape. The instructor and trainees were present with the aircraft which was well fuelled. Above all, the weather was fantastic. So, as usual, the training captain went into the rhetoric of the training flight's pre-departure briefing after which the routine statement that signified the end of a briefing (i.e. did anybody have a question) was made. The instructor then continued, now on an individual basis, to ask technical questions about the aircraft so as to ascertain the depth of our knowledge of the aircraft. After satisfying himself, we then boarded the aircraft.

The training started. By law, we were required do fly a minimum of six take-offs and six landings duly ratified by the training captain before the CAA stamped the aircraft type rating on the crew member's licence. The training was a bit rough for all of us due to our not having flown for a while, and also, naturally, we encountered the usual problems involved in learning to fly new equipment.

I eventually got my endorsement after flying a total of six and a half hours on the aircraft. The next phase for me now was to revalidate my instrument endorsement. The normal validity of the instrument endorsement was thirteen months from the date the instrument flight check was conducted.

My instrument check was conducted on a normal passenger flight. It was my first experience in passenger flying. All along, it had been an encounter with one instructor or another. I did the check with the authorised instrument FCAA examiner, Captain J C Roy, and the normal two-man cockpit crew members on board the service. The service was WT 613, with Captain Makpo as the rostered captain. The examiner had a seat provided him to enable him to witness and make an on-the-spot assessment of my flight test. It was a check where I had to put in all I had learnt on the aircraft and demonstrate a maximum application of my knowledge the same way I would be required to in the presence of fare paying passengers who were entitled to the crew's smooth discharge of the services they had paid for.

From the onset, I already had the natural butterflies-in-the-stomach feeling that quite a large percentage of cockpit crew members normally went through during any type of flight check. The reason for this will be discussed later in this book. Another rather discouraging factor that day was the fact that all the three guys who had gone through this same check ahead of me failed, and to make matters worse, they had talked so much about having done their best, but it seemed that the examiner had been expecting an astronaut-type performance. As much as the news was not the best, as an individual I had come to learn the hard way that you might listen to all sorts of comments from people, but opinion formation on the particular subject matter remained your sole prerogative. So I went for the flight check with equitable caution and full of determination to succeed (whether as pilot or astronaut), and to face the examiner, and not the personality.

It was so simple. The instrument check was a very straight-forward test in that the test required you to manipulate the aircraft by strict reference to the aircraft instruments throughout the prescribed manoeuvre recommended by the examiner. All the instruments are visibly located in the pilot's forward field of vision in the cockpit. As a matter of fact, it is one check I usually refer to as "what-you-fly-is-what-you-get check". The examiner's pronouncement of the check outcome in an ideal situation (i.e. devoid of bias) is just an official confirmation of the outcome you, the candidate, had arrived at in your mind on completion of the check.

I rode with the examiner and passed, too. I knew, while the check was in progress, that I wasn't faring badly. So being informed by the examiner that I passed the check was no big surprise to me, but what I don't know, even now, is whether that made me an astronaut. If it did, then I congratulate myself on being the first in Africa, even ahead of the more experienced examiner himself.

In summary, all these prerequisites (required by both the CAA and the air carrier itself) were what new pilots had to accomplish before the company could pronounce them productive second officers. It was this status of second officer that gave significance and recognition to any crew member's names on the crew roster.

One major requirement, also, was the fitness test. I have earlier discussed this while discussing the initial flight school training. The fitness test, though not different from the flight school fitness check format, was an entirely different ball game for the majority of pilots (including me), in career flying. Ipso facto, I shall quickly reflect on this issue strictly as a matter of personal opinion.

The Medical Fitness Check

The career pilot, by law, must have in his possession a CPL with an instrument rating endorsement on it before he can carry passengers for commercial purposes or hire. It's a pilot's trade certificate. Civil aviation authorities globally, having taken cognisance of the high risk involved in aircraft operations, have made the safety factor in flight operations their most vital area of concern. One of the policies adopted is making sure that the pilot who plays a vital role in aircraft operations is certified medically fit. Emphasis on the fitness of crew members is reflected in the half-yearly pilgrimage crew members make for fitness assessment throughout their career. The fitness test that was so natural, simple, and quite easy to me in the days spent in flight training school suddenly became some sort of terrifying experience after I had completed a decade in commercial aviation. This resulted from the natural and logical fear of being certified unfit to fly. The pilot is a skilled professional, with this rather rigid skill being his only bargaining power. So with his single economic base, it is obvious that without the opportunity to apply his skill, he will have no other lawful means of livelihood. Secondly, he is only too aware of the harsh realities of his being just another human being. He knows that he is susceptible to any phenomena on the planet Earth and that no man yet has got total biological control of his life and existence. Human health management depends primarily on nature, but with advancement in medical science man (including the pilot) has been able to achieve the rather commendable feat of a relatively low mortality rate. But in spite of this achievement medical science still remains at the mercy of nature.

There is a common saying that "health is wealth". This saying, in a nutshell, is what the career span of a pilot is all about. Since good health in a pilot's career is also good wealth, if nature fails him health-wise, then there goes the wealth as well, as far as flying is concerned. It is this that makes pilots like me regard the half-yearly fitness pilgrimage as a date to keep with fate. Even after succeeding in this pilgrimage for over fourteen years, I still reserve my sincere respect for nature and to obviate any form of induced anxiety that may lead to failure in the check, I try my best to put into use vital medical information that may be of great help in mitigating this "collywobbly feeling'" (as the Americans would call it).

The interesting part of the whole scenario is the fact that once the check gets started all the butterfly anxiety just fizzles out. I am of the opinion that the antidote against this "white collar hypertension" lies in the hospitality and fellow-feeling of the hand conducting the test. So far in my career, I have found out that to a large extent the doctors conducting the test can influence the outcome. The test itself is a printed format delineating specifically the areas of importance to the CAA about the candidate. To end the session, I hate the unknown, so figuring my opinion about the check is as easy as Sunday morning.

There ends the making of a productive second officer. Everything is now in place. The next sojourn is going through the indoctrination process that would finally qualify one for upgrading to the position of a first officer.

The Making of a First Officer

Different airlines all over the world adopt different lines of indoctrination that suit the aims and objectives of the company and still remain in accordance with the governing laws of the aviation industry. The main objective of the training is for the trainee to accomplish standardisation in practice, behaviour and terminology. In Nigeria Airways, the trainee, by policy, would have to do a minimum of 100 hours of flight time, and if found suitable he would then be recommended for a flight check.

A line training flight is a schedule airline service with or without passengers aboard, where the trainee is allowed to manipulate the controls of the aircraft under the supervision of the captain. The captain's role in the process remains an autocratic one. According to aviation laws and in consensus with the aircraft manufacturers, it is assumed that during any flight operations the captain is always at the controls of the aircraft. This is what is referred to as the captain being in command of the flight. The captain is entrusted with the overall safe operation of the aircraft in all phases of flight. He is absolutely in charge of both the aircraft and the crew members.

The trainee continues to hold a borderline status throughout his line indoctrination training because by law the airline will assume responsibility for redelegation of tasks. Since the trainee is delegated to manipulate the aircraft controls, in any eventuality under this arrangement the airline in concert with the captain is liable.

This policy adopted by aviation authorities and aircraft manufacturers (though predicated on the safety factor) has continued to be the grey area (amongst others) in flight execution especially for trainees. This sometimes turns the line training into a big drag. My line indoctrination training on the F27, started on the 31st of October, 1980, under the command of Captain Sanger (an Indian) on service WT 401/4 with a routing from Lagos, via Ibadan and Kaduna with a turnaround in Kano, then back through Jos to Ibadan before finally proceeding to Lagos. The flight's termination in Lagos signified the end of a day's job. On that service we had on board another new intake, but this time a captain, and an Indian, by the name of Manoher. Since Captain Sanger happened to be a line training captain, he could choose to occupy any active crew seat in the cockpit. That day, he occupied the right seat in the cockpit which is the bona fide seat of the first officer while Captain Manoher occupied the left seat.

During the flight, I came to realise that both of them were the same tribesmen from India. They were a great pair and I really enjoyed flying with them. Apart from radio communications between us and the air traffic control (which conventionally is in the English language) the guys communicated with each other throughout the flight in their native tongue thereby leaving me out of the cockpit's communication gossip loop. When they were not engaged in tale telling, Manoher made use of the interlude to sing some songs which were probably top of the chart in India then. He had arrived from India only two weeks before this flight, which presumably made him current on events at home. In all honesty, Manoher possessed a rather melodious voice. While he sang, Sanger just kept shaking his head in admiration. I was stuck with listening to varieties of Indian top of the pops for seven hours. But I still can't remember having heard any of these songs on MTV or any other universal top ten charts in pop music. I guess that's probably why Manoher chose flying as a profession instead of a musical career.

By virtue of the roster, I was stuck with these pair of fine, experienced and skilful professionals for thirteen consecutive days. In that time, we operated a total of seven different schedule services. I learnt a whole lot from this pair, and logged a total flight training of thirty-five hours during the span of my thirteen-day operation with them. They were so nice and understanding that they allowed me more than nine hours of practice in manipulating the aircraft controls as part of my thirty-five hours flight time logged in line training. Suffice it to mention here that this unique act of magnanimity was rare, especially during line training for green second officers. Many captains consider it a risk to delegate flight duties to a green second officer.

After the thirteen-day stint with my Indian friends, I continued my training with another captain from the Philippines, named Valerio. He wasn't the only Filipino on the F27 fleet then; there was another one called Gim, who also was a captain. Captain Valerio, apart from being a training captain, was a highly skilful professional. He worked so hard that he could tell you the number of bolts holding the structure of the F27 aircraft together. He, I would say, got me fully "disvirginised" on the F27 as far as the skill of handling the aircraft was concerned. Unfortunately, I only operated five services with him before I went to do my flight check for the purpose of being upgraded to the position of a substantive First Officer (F/O). In the process of accomplishing my F27 line training, I had flown with a roll-call of five captains (Sanger, Valerio, Gim, Okandeji, Oyedeji), over a period of exactly three months. Having logged a total of 112 hours of line training in the process, I was recommended and subsequently scheduled for the flight check. This schedule was the golden opportunity to finally divorce myself from the servility of being a second officer. If I was successful it would be "uhuru" (freedom) at last.

As an F/O the pattern of relationship regarding one's rank within the airline community changes. You are now second in command to a captain and so some measure of authority is now reposed in you. Shakespeare once said that "every man enjoys that brief moment of his authority". I believe that to be very true indeed. The difference in status between the second officer and the F/O is quite immense. This is reflected in the roles already established by the governing authority's laws and is further polished by the air carrier's (or the company's) policy. Taking the indices one by one, a substantive F/O is a mandatory entity in the cockpit crew composition. He is so mandatory that without him the captain cannot legally fly the aircraft. Also, he has all the required legal backing from the aviation authority to keep the captain in check as politely as possible, if need be. Also once the F/O has proved himself an able backup to the captain by demonstrating a combination of proficient skill and humility, it is almost certain that the key to the captain's box of experience and know-how, advice and magnanimity would become his. He needn't be the hypocrite, flatterer, time server, or worshipper of tyrants. But the second officer is at the mercy of both the captain and the co-pilot. Once, when a captain and his co-pilot were discussing an issue that vitally affected an aircraft's flight, a director of flight operations at the Nigeria Airways said the time had not come for a second officer to open his mouth.

The second officer had wanted to make a contribution. Although the director's rebuke appears an extreme example and devoid of foresight, it nevertheless gives an insight into the lowly regard usually accorded second officers.

So it can easily be seen that climbing up in the hierarchy from second to first officer made a hell of a difference!

All in a Day's Job for the Pilot

I will use the flight I operated on my flight check for my upgrading from second officer to substantive F/O to illustrate a day's job primarily as a worker and then as a pilot in Nigeria Airways. The pilot, as a professional in an airline, practically speaking plays the leading role in the chain of motion of an airline. Sometimes, a crew member's sudden realisation of his unique and immense importance usually leads to the undesirable exhibition of professional arrogance. This, in my own opinion, is a natural tendency which must be under reasonable control as much as possible. As a matter of personal opinion, my submission in quotes is, "sat sapienti" ("enough for a wise man").

A rostered crew member reporting for duty presumably has in his possession valid certificates that make it legal for him to operate in whatever capacity he is employed. In an airline structure, the pilot is a shift-worker. By virtue of his training, he is qualified to work at any time of the day. So, he may report for duty day or night, depending on his roster. In reporting for duty (as a reasonable and social being) he is under obligation to have no doubts about his condition of health and professional proficiency.

The policy in Nigeria Airways regarding crew members reporting for duty requires them to mandatorily arrive at the airport at least an hour before the scheduled departure time for their service. As a matter of principle, as long as a crew member is not on leave, his day-to-day activities are centred upon his roster schedule in such a way that his readiness for duty is entirely predicated on the scheduled departure time. In effect, for a rostered early morning departure day and for a night departure, his readiness starts as early as the early part of that day. This way he is able to divorce himself long enough from all human activities by resting so as to achieve maximum alertness at reporting time. Being alert is one of the important tools of work in flying and this has been my personal approach and has proved quite efficacious. In my fourteen years in Nigeria Airways, I can easily claim above 90% average in reporting for duty on schedule. This principle is based on my family upbringing, and beyond that, having lived in different western societies, I have come to appreciate the essence of time. As the saying goes, responsibility is obedience in a special direction. This made me adopt this approach to life generally.

On the 31st of January, 1981, I was still very much a bona fide member of the Lagos Society of Pedestrians which membership assigned to one the day-to-day onerous task of patronising public transport to and from work. After two and a half years of this, the situation became a reluctantly accepted routine. On the day in question, I reported for work dead on schedule. I recall that that afternoon, some colleagues of mine who also reported for work found the parking lot provided for pilots quite useful. In my case, I wasn't that lucky, because I had no personal car. A few guys in my set were lucky enough to have benefited from the airline's car loan scheme for pilots and flight engineers. The rest of us were unlucky. We were a pre-SAP (Structural Adjustment Programme) set and yet were not lucky then, not to mention when SAP came into effect. Remember that SAP involved the introduction of belt-tightening measures by the government, and Nigeria Airways was (and still is) a government parastatal.

What made me feel quite unhappy about the whole thing was the fact that I was only two names away on the car loan scheme list before it got abolished. I was two steps away because of two odds against me. Firstly, the age factor, and secondly, an alphabetical advantage. Why? Well, we were a set of nine individuals and we all joined the company at the same time. So in determining priority among us, age and the alphabetical order of our names were the criteria used. Once again, letters of the alphabet mysteriously became a source of inequality. Who says that all things are not at the mercy of Mother Nature?

Luckily, towards the end of 1981, I was able to afford my own car through my own private resources. Among my set, the longest serving pedestrian (name withheld) bought his first car in October, 1991. I learnt two lessons here. One, as a civil servant, whatever role you play in the service must be based on the sincere premise that you love to serve the public, and secondly, all thoughts of any form of substantial pecuniary reward should be totally suppressed. The civil service remuneration structure is just good enough to sustain your existence thereby keeping you alive and able to come to work. The pilot in the civil service structure is just a glorified driver so to speak. He has no special remuneration as a consideration for the nature of his job and his skill.

Even the supposedly glorified driver thing is just a cosmetic term. The glorification is only in your occasionally ferrying the societal elite, the "timbers and calibres" and so on, who all enjoy sitting in the cockpit. My deduction after several personal encounters with them is that while they are there with you in the cockpit, they are all quite articulate in the rhetoric of flattery for the cockpit crew, and ready with the usual "is that so?" statement of pity, well meshed with a derisive look, when you mention how unhappy you are with the company and the government because of your poor salary. The usual pretended ignorance of this issue would make one conclude that all these people probably attended the same institution for cockpit crew flattery. This flattery is always of very high resonance while the airplane is airborne. Then as soon as the aircraft is parked, the feigned pity disappears only to resurface once more in the form of a pecuniary gift. As for me, I feel a bit nauseated any time this happens because the money means that your complaint has been equated to the plea of a beggar, and has failed to achieve positive progress for the sake of posterity.

I recall that shortly after I had become a captain, I had one of these ex-excellencies on board my flight one day. As usual, he ended up riding in the cockpit with us, went through the same storyline, and finally, as expected, came out with his own donation. I recall the gentleman donating the sum of N5,000 to us. Little did he realise that his generous gift as far as I was concerned became a springboard for me to finally try (at least) to correct the impression his type had formed that our complaint about our pittance of an income had nothing to do with pecuniary donations. I recall thanking the excellency, politely refusing the donation and going on to solicit his assistance in lobbying the right quarters to correct this anomaly, instead of this rather unsteady gift custom that depended largely on luck. I pleaded for a generally improved remuneration package that would benefit our professional fold.

In Nigeria Airways, a pilot reports for duty dressed in a white shirt, a pair of black trousers, black shoes, black tie, and a black cap. Fully dressed, the pilot now carries his working tools, i.e. navigation charts, navigation computer, writing pen, a serviceable flashlight, a calculator and other necessary items that would enhance the smooth execution of his flight. All these, are carried in a bag, commonly referred to as the "Flight Bag".

With my flight bag, I reported for duty at the dispatch office of the flight operations department located at the local wing of the Murtala Muhammed Airport, Ikeja, Lagos. As soon as you approach the kiosk-like structure, one major activity that confirms your being in the right office is the festival of noise from radio transmission boxes and their operators, the dispatchers themselves and the operating crew traffic requesting different information. Sometimes, your voice has to be at the highest pitch with the dispatcher countering too at his loudest so as to establish the normal two-way communication. That afternoon of the 31st of June, 1981, I formed a part of the noise festival as I looked up at the big whiteboard that displayed all information about the flights scheduled for the day. I was quite happy that my name was reflected along with the two cockpit operating crew, with the abbreviation R/C (meaning "route check") written in front of it. I thanked God that so far there was no discrepancy. Speaking of the dispatch office, it was a square space, and the first form of wall decoration was the big whiteboard, placed in such a way that any person not suffering from myopia would see it at once on entering the office. The board reflected technical information about flight operations for the day. One could refer to it as the situation board for flight operations. Apart from it, different bills were posted all around the walls containing additional information which might be useful to the crew. The rest of the office space was furnished with the usual office desks and chairs. There were shelves filled with navigational logs for the company's route web.

Outside the common standard of civilised behaviour of having exchanged greetings with the duty dispatchers, the first dispatch departure formality of a pilot was to acquaint himself with the NOTAMS file (the acronym NOTAMS means Notice To Airmen). This file contains outstanding information relating to all stations and areas within the company's route web. This file is kept valid and updated by the NOTAMS section of the company's flight technical services. Understanding all updated information in this file is a big stock-in-trade in flight execution and also an insurance against professional embarrassment. Lack of vital and updated information is unvenial in aviation and also a negligent and criminal dereliction of statutory duty. It is an act of a tortfeasor.

Since the day's flight happened to be a flight check in nature for me and more so one whose completion would upgrade me to the position of an F/O, then for today and until the end of the flight I would be operating in the capacity of a nascent and physically imaginary first officer. In this case, everything pertaining to the operation of this flight would be my responsibility for the duration of the flight. This day I was strictly on my own. Before the legally rostered crew reported at the dispatch office, I had already started performing the pre-departure duty of the F/O, as far as the role of the F/O on the ground was concerned. This entailed my getting in concert with the dispatcher in charge of the de facto service.

A qualified dispatcher in an airline structure is the principal assistant to the captain on ground. One may start wondering then about the position and role of the F/O while on ground too. The difference in a nutshell is that the dispatcher as a worker, is of specialised skill too. By virtue of his training he has gone through the whole pilot's ground training syllabus, from the Private Pilot's License (PPL) to the most advanced Airline Transport License course (ATPL). He has also done this in more depth and detail than the pilot. So while on ground he is able to gather vast information with regards to a particular flight, assess this information, or sometimes get the information interlarded, in such a way that his admonition to the captain during briefing is quite clear and devoid of any ambiguity as much as possible. This way, he may then claim the role reposed in him by the company. His assistance terminates as soon as the dispatch departure briefing is over. From this point onwards, the F/O takes over the mantle of assistantship in flight execution. Also, he takes over this role on the ground, he must have been in touch with both the captain and the duty dispatcher, and if need be make inputs as per the flight. His consent as per the briefing is also quite important. As I was just getting in rhythm with the dispatcher, the captain walked into the office. Of course the dispatcher's attention shifted to him. He then started briefing him. The dispatcher briefs on a flight by following an already prepared format reflected on the briefing sheet printed and arranged by the printing department of the company under the strict guidelines of the company's flight operations experts. The format includes information like aircraft registration, aircraft gross weight and total payload for the service, the service number itself (in our case it was WT 251), the departure field, the destination, the alternate destination field in case for any unforeseeable reason the flight cannot land at the planned destination airport, passenger number, captain's name, and so on. While the captain was being briefed, I stood next to him, listening with rapt attention, as the company's policy requires of the F/O.

At the end of the briefing, the captain turned around and asked me if I had any questions, or anything to contribute. As for that flight, I had none. All this while (since reporting and since the arrival of the captain, I kept wondering why the F/O hadn't reported yet, because from my knowledge of his attitude he never

DEPARTURE

	TR MAG	DIST NM	B733	B707	A310	DC10	F/P TIME	CUM TIME	WAYPT FACILITY	IHS	COORD	ATC FREQ	AK WAY	MCA	CR FL
	045	56	12	08	08	08			LO 113.7	N05 E003	426 166	TWR 118.1 APP 124.3	UR 78D	3.8	0
									IB 112.1		208 580				

ENROUTE

	059	44	09	06	06	06			UTA						
	059	118	17	16	16	16			BD 112.7	N06 E006	355 050			3.4	
	045	122	09	17	17	17			KU 114.7	N07 N02	355 022	APP 124.1 113.1	UR 77B		
	040	106	18	16	16	16			KA 112.5	N08 N08	215				
		446	1.11	1.65	1.05	1.05			DNKN 1565						

ARRIVAL

							AUR (1)		LAGOS						
	220	106	17	16	16	16			KA 112.5	N12 E008	022 208	TWR 118.1 APP 124.1	UR 77B	3.4	B
	225	122	19	18	18	18			KU 114.7	N10 N07	022 223				
	259	118	18	17	17	17			BE 112.7	E95 E05	090		UR 728D		
	259	44	07	06	06	06			IB 112.1	N07 N03	208 580	APP 124.3 TWR 113.1	UR 778	3.8	
	225	56	10	09	09	09			LO 113.7	N09 N05	426 166				
		7	02	02	02	02			DNKN 135'	N06 E003	245 191				
		55	1.19	1.10	1.10	1.10									

TIME		
CHOCK ON	LAND	
CHOCK OF	T/O	
BLOCK TIME	FLT TIME	

CRUISE LEVELS	FUEL	B737	B707	A310	DC10
	FLIGHT	4000	7600	6000	10500
B.737:	CONT	400	3500	1600	2900
B.707:	ALT	4000	6600	5000	10000
A.310:	HOLD	2100	2500	3700	3500
DC.10:	TAXY	200	500	400	700
CAPTAIN DISPR	SECTOR	10700	20700	16700	27200
ISSUE DATE	MIN R.T.F				

A Typical Navigational Log

came late to work) the first officer's absence was still in my mind as we were about to leave the office. The captain, as a matter of confirmation, inquired if I had collected the navigational log for the trip. To this I answered in the affirmative. I was so glad leaving that office at least. As much as the office is a vital substratum unit in flight operations, noise seems to be the catalyst of information. But before I move on, I shall quickly explain what the navigational log is all about. It is in short, a rectangular piece of paper, printed specifically for the service being operated. In our own case, our service (WT 251) was an Enugu-bound service. So, for the purpose of clarity, the flight leg, or routing, is always reflected at the top right-hand corner of the paper, co-located with the type of equipment (in our case, it was the F27) being used for that particular service. This is so because most of the navigational information reflected on the log is entirely predicated on the aircraft performance and her characteristics. Other information, such as the originator of the document and date of printing, amongst others that I shall mention soon, are all reflected, with each and every detail having a vital role in enhancing the overall smooth and safe execution of the flight.

To show the importance of this document, it is required by law to file the document after completion of flight for a period of six months from date of operation. Before I delve into the importance of the rest of the information on this paper not mentioned yet, let's look objectively into the three indicia I have already mentioned. Our flight was to go to Enugu (from Lagos) and back. In effect the information at the right-hand corner of the paper should reflect Lagos to Enugu (usually, on the form it is reflected as LOS/ENU-F27) then the originator of the document, i.e. Nigeria Airways, is clearly written at the top left-hand corner. Then boldly written too is the title of the form. Now the importance and also the need for these mentioned indicia so far is that, let's say for example, and hypothetically too, that a crew member reports for duty, and the dispatcher as part of his duty hands him a navigational log for LOS/MIU/IKAD/LOS, (but the crew is scheduled for a service to LOS/CBQ/PHC/LOS) and innocently for judicial reasons (vis-à-vis having worked with the dispatch office for over a reasonable time so far and flawlessly too, and given room for this routine behaviour to manifest into a state of complacency in him) he decides not to check the documents, then legally it is a clear-cut case of negligence of duty by both parties, one contributory, and the other just a clear-cut one. As for the originator, if the company as the originator has not hired the service of the originator, that is, as in charter contracts, it would be a felony for this document to be found in use by another operator.

In brief, these are the legal aspects of these particularly discussed indicia. Also this document is a good source of information in the investigation of a reportable incident or an accident (if found) in the sense that it complements both the voice and flight recorders, thereby consequently simplifying the onerous task of an incident/accident investigator. Instead of making the rest of the information in this document as dry and forbidding as the Mojave or the Sahara desert, I shall make a metaphorical summation of the information. So let's look at it this way. Let's say one has a computer, and in the computer one stored a long profile of information, in such a way that some result or a specific result is expected from the information profile stored. But for some reason during the storage of this information there was some erroneous information already stored but which you didn't detect, then of course if you now select on the computer's menu that particular information profile, the computer of course will give a profile based on the wrong information input you made. Then surely the profile will be different from your expected result. Just like the general and reluctant gripe of computer owners, "garbage in, garbage out". The only undesirable aspect about this is that in flight execution, this may be very disastrous. In summary, flying or the execution of it is a form or a department of science itself. That is to say if the right procedure is followed, the right result will certainly be achieved. Conversely the wrong procedure will certainly evolve into a wrong result.

Well, I had the right navigational log with me, so thus far things were going the right way. But still the absence of the F/O and the reason for it was now very much inchoate to me, but the fact that the captain didn't even seem to be bothered gave me a surmised scintilla of the whole flight check, the least of which will be cancellation of the service due to non-appearance of the rostered F/O. Captain Valerio (now my check captain) is a base training instructor, and by virtue of this he is legally in order by law to conduct a passenger service with any type-rated crew on the aircraft. So, as far as the crew composition was concerned, we were legal to fly. While we were walking towards the airplane, I looked at her green and white colour, and the company's logo at the tail of the airplane. Then suddenly I decided to have a look into my small book that contains the glossary of the characteristics of each and all the F27 airplanes we had on the fleet. During line training I used the different airplane registrations to compile my small book. That day, the airplane registration was 5N-ANT, so I opened my book to that page, then under the subtitle "Glossary", I immediately refreshed my mind about the idiosyncrasies of the airplane. In my glossary book, I named all the different aircraft after different names, most of whom were captains on the fleet and the rest F/Os. This way, I was easily able to refresh my mind about that personality and consequently the airplane. It's a pity I will not be able to reveal the name I gave to 5N-ANT. All I can say is that during my line training I did most of my training on this airplane, and I enjoyed any time I was allowed to fly it. So at least things are still in order so far.

As we continued our walk to the airplane, the captain turned around to me and said, "Ty, I know how you feel today, but I must tell you. I have flown long enough with you during your line training, and I was quite impressed with your progress. So do me a favour, just relax and be yourself." Still talking, he said, "I am even ready to sign your papers before the flight. But I must tell you that by law you and I know that I cannot do that. So just do your job the way you have been doing it and with luck everything will be okay. Remember, everybody is waiting for the outcome of your check, though you might not know this. I am just telling you from experience. Also if you goof, I would not hesitate to flunk you."

Right after that, we went into the cross-examination of the airplane's technical details. The prosecutor was just about getting into full rhythm when we suddenly arrived at the foot of the airplane's airstairs. There, I met the rostered F/O, standing and

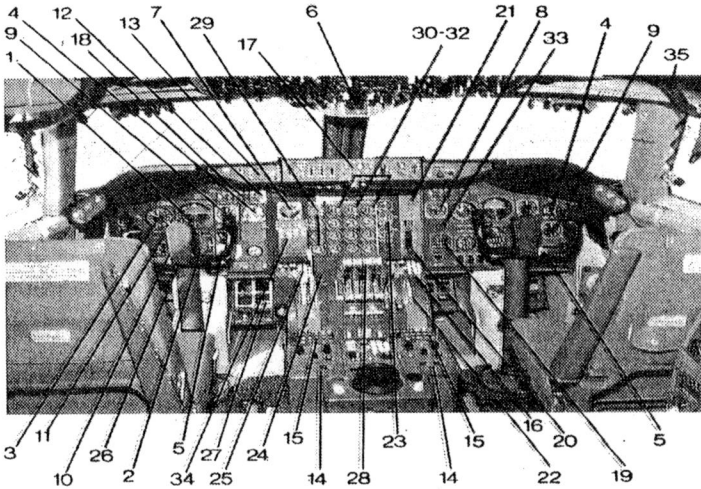

1	director horizon	18	a/p and flight director mode indicators
2	flight compass		
3	airspeed indicator	19	a/p trim indicators
4	altimeter	20	undercarriage selector
5	vertical speed indicator	21	undercarriage lights
6	magnetic compass	22	flap selector
7	standby horizon	23	flap position indicator
8	standby altimeter	24	airbrake selector
9	radio altimeter	25	stabilator trim
10	radio magnetic indicator	26	flying controls
11	distance measuring equipment (DME)	27	rudder pedals
		28	throttles
12	marker lights	29	engine instruments number one engine
13	VHF navigation frequency		
14	VHF communications frequency selector	30–32	engine instruments numbers 2–4 engines
15	radio selector box	33	outside air temperature
16	inertial navigation system (INS)	34	central warning system
17	autopilot (a/p)	35	smoke and oxygen masks

Typical Jetliner Cockpit Instrument Panel

smiling at me sheepishly. I greeted him, then the captain and I walked past him and embarked the airplane. Now, the first function the cockpit crew perform the moment they enter the airplane prepared for service is to acquaint themselves with the serviceability of the airplane. This procedure by law is performed by making reference to the airplane's Technical Log Book. This in aviation is simply referred to as the "tech-log". This booklet, so to speak, is analogous to the case file of a hospital patient in the sense that the booklet contains all information (in technical details) about the airplane, i.e. date of manufacture (which is reminiscent of a human being's date of birth), hours flown since date of manufacture (i.e. like the age of a man), etc., but the area of importance to the pilot in this booklet is the column where all the technical snags (or ailments) are entered. This column, coupled with the ability to interpret the entries made therein, in strict consultation (meticulously too) with other engineering dispatch technical booklets, i.e. the Minimum Equipment List and the Configuration Deviation List, aids the captain to easily assess and crystallise all the entries made in that column so that he can reach a constructive and conclusive decision about the serviceability of the airplane in accordance with the law, taking cognisance of the responsibility reposed in him in his capacity as the *pilot in command*. This process and the outcome of the captain's decision is a major event in the final dispatch of a service. In short, this area is highly combustible. It is in this area that the captain must absolutely make sure that his professional thought process and final judgement are of value and absolutely "on the money" and in order.

Also, as in common law, apart from the fact that the co-pilot is a legal entity in flight execution, it is natural for him to disagree with the captain's decision sometimes if in his own professional opinion he finds the captain's judgement unsafe, since he is still entitled to his legal right to personal safety. I shall later on in this book explain in full detail how much this area in flight dispatch has come to be highly politicised with the result that any adverse but sincere legal decision of the crew on the vicarious liability of the captain is sometimes seen as an act of sabotage. Indeed, sometimes suspicion of brain infirmity could be alleged.

Speculation of deliberate hatred for a certain professional group may even be imputed, and so on and so forth.

Well, for our service that day the airplane was in order. That took care of the technical log and the drama that goes with it sometimes. The next task was the external pre-flight check or, simply put, external walk around the airplane. This task is performed by both cockpit crew, simply because in the law of safety it is believed that two heads are better than one. The nature of this task requires the crew members to ascertain that the overall airplane structure externally is in one piece. The walk pattern to be followed is very well sketched and also outlined in the aircraft operations manual. The pattern emphasises the need to check some part of the airplane surface for damages, or in some cases for missing components too, and also to check for fluid leaks around any of the airplane structure that forms part of a fluid piped system and structure. In the process of following the walk pattern, one would have made a complete circle around the airplane. If on completion of this everything is found intact the crew then proceeds back to the airplane.

Entering the cockpit, the task is now bifurcated by regulations and enhanced by prescribed procedure. The bottom line in flight execution is being able to adhere strictly and proficiently to these procedures. In brief, procedure is the great flywheel of flight execution, in that it divides clearly crew members' workload and fixes their responsibility accordingly without any room for ambiguity. So by procedure as F/O, the next task was to make sure that all the emergency equipment in the cockpit was in place and also labelled valid and serviceable. After this, I then continued in a scan flow pattern, to check the serviceability of the airplane systems by turning the systems' switch on and off, thereby activating and deactivating the systems. Tests on some systems are tactile, while some are just a matter of visual confirmation. This task phase is called the preliminary cockpit preparation or set-up. With every check performed so far in order, I now commenced the final cockpit preparation and simultaneously requested for boarding of passengers on the captain's order. While I was busy performing my own task, the captain was also on his own side of the cockpit performing his checks by strictly following the procedure check format. On completion of his check, he now by procedure again requested for the before-start checklist. Before I go on, it is necessary for me to once and for all explain here that in the operation of airplanes generally, the booklet used to confirm and also delineate the procedure the crew member may have to carry out under certain conditions is referred to as the *checklist*. Basically, reading of the checklist is the sole responsibility of the first officer, but sometimes if the pilot at the controls happens to be the F/O, the captain, now in his role as pilot not flying (PNF), would at certain phases of flight be saddled with the task of reading the checklist. Also, the pilot, by virtue of his training, does a lot of actions by recall, with the prescribed and the recommended procedure coupled with the format, sequence and pattern to follow as his guideline. So far, the concept of the use of the checklist, and ability of the crew member in attaining the standard required in performing some of his duties solely by recall, has proved very efficacious in flight execution. One may want to ask why one has to depend on human memory that is naturally prone to nature due to the human factor involved. Well, the need for memory actions lies in the harsh fact that there are some forms of emergency that may confront the crew during the flight in such a way that if crew response is not spontaneous to the situation, that time impasse may lead to loss of valuable lives, or sometimes colossal damage to the equipment itself. This handbook (the checklist) is a dual-purpose booklet. Since the main purpose of the book is to specifically aid the crew in carrying out their specific duties procedure-wise, the application of the book's contents then is a continuous process for the entire duration of a flight. Also, the book carries vast operational information that the crew may need to make quick reference to, instead of having to go through the airplane operations manual, which may be time-wasting and sometimes costly to the smooth execution of the flight.

The booklet also contains formats under different titles for both normal and abnormal situations (forming the major bifurcated text). Since every action and procedure is carried out as per the checklist format, I went ahead and read the before-start checklist, as requested by the captain. This checklist phase ensures that the completion of all actions we had performed by reference to memory had actually been achieved. Reading the checklist is a form of interrogation process where the crew reading the checklist items listens out for the right response from the crew being interrogated, and also makes a visual confirmation of those actions being done correctly. It is entirely forbidden, both in practice and by law, to read the checklist by rote. Apart from this being an act of misfeasance, it shows criminal complacency of the particular crew, and an undesirable disregard of statutorily recommended procedure. It also shows the crew's sordidness or ignorance of the safety factor in flight execution.

Some crew members to this day in day-to-day operations commit in my own opinion this very serious offence. This probably emanates from the simple fact that, after a long period of repetitive usage of the checklist, the tendency is that the whole process becomes routine and consequently the temptation of rote action becomes a habit. From my experience, and globally too, I have witnessed crew members commit this offence to the extent that for a borderline professional this offence is one of the numerous peccadilloes that occur in everyday flight execution.

Apart from the fact that I was under check, I have never in my career to date formed the bad habit of default in any recommended flight procedure or manoeuvre. As for my de facto flight, I continued the long sing song like reading the before-start checklist, until I got to the item on the list that says "papers", of which the desirable response from the captain should have been "aboard". But here, he responded by saying "Standby," which meant that the paper in question was not aboard. This paper is the document referred to in aviation as the load sheet. Again this is another vital document by law that must also be safely filed away for six months from the date of flight operation (in case of any eventuality).

The document carries information, such as (1) passenger figures and their cumulative gross weight; (2) amount of fuel on board the airplane; (3) cargo weight or load if any, etc. The importance of this is to ascertain that the aircraft has been properly loaded, and if that is the case, then the airplane's centre of gravity would be in the safe envelope thereby assuring the stability of the airplane in all axes. As soon as the captain received the paper, scrutinised it, and then endorsed it, he told me to continue with the checklist. Of course I had to repeat that item once more, and this time I got the right response of "aboard". The captain then asked me to request start-up clearance for Enugu from Lagos Air Traffic Control (ATC) unit and this was granted. The universally accepted language of communication between an airplane station and the ATC unit is the English language. To request start-up clearance one has to put into use the standard phraseology and terminology because the progenitors of aviation have worked so hard in making sure that aviation words are strictly object words, the syntax of which makes an object language or phrase completely devoid of any ambiguity. To ensure the mastery of this radio telephony language you must have gone through the course on this, completion of which would earn you a radio telephony license. Without this license, it is absolutely illegal to operate an airplane radio station. As the saying goes, education is the vehicle of civilisation. So also is humility the vehicle of harmonious communication with the ATC unit. So my request conversation went like this.

WT 251: "Lagos tower, good afternoon, this is WT 251."

Lagos tower: "WT 251, good afternoon and go ahead."

WT 251: "WT 251 requests airfield data and start-up clearance. Destination Enugu. Position local ramp."

Lagos tower: "WT 251 Lagos at 1200Z. Wind: 210/05 kts, CAVOK. Temperature: 32, QNH: 1012. Runway in use: 19L. Cleared to start for Enugu, and call when ready for taxi."

W. T. 251: "Roger, Lagos tower. Temperature: 32, QNH: 1012, runway 19L in use, cleared to start for Enugu, will call you when ready to taxi."

Lagos tower: "Roger, WT 251."

With the airfield data he had just given me, I now went into the airplane's Take-Off Performance Chart. Using the given temperature, I now entered the column for our airplane's take-off gross weight as reflected in the load sheet to compute the take-off speeds with an option of the flap setting of my choice, which was 16½. Aircraft speeds are abbreviated to the letter V and are referred to as V speeds. The speeds of concern for a pilot attempting a take-off, are: (1) The engine failure recognition speed, or the decision speed. Known as V1; (2) The airplane rotation speed: Vr; (3) The airplane take-off safety speed: V2.

The F27 has a unique speed feature in the sense that the V1 and Vr speeds are the same. This reduces the performance workload of the co-pilot as far as speed computation is concerned. I now completed the card. We normally enter this computed speed with the rest of the necessary information already inserted in the card known as the bug card. This I handed over to the captain, firstly, for him to verify if the speed was right. If so, he then uses his white bug air speed cursor to set the computed speed on his air speed indicator for enhanced visual reference during the take-off roll. I also did the same on my own air speed indicator. Suffice it to mention here that the cockpit's instrumentation is dually installed, that is to say, whatever component installed on the captain's panel is also installed on the co-pilot's panel too. This way, whichever pilot controls the airplane does so solely by reference to the instrument directly installed in his forward field vision. This panel is called the instrument panel. It is one amongst numerous panels that form the cockpit structure. The panel is the most active interface in flight execution in the sense that, throughout the duration of flight, the crew members continue to make manual inputs on the panel. As a matter of fact, sometimes inputs made on this panel at a certain phase of flight betoken the need for making reference to and reading the checklist regarding that input. Before the airplane starts to leave the parking ramp (i.e. taxi) inputs would have been made manually by the crew member procedurally on different and necessary panels for the flight phase at that point in time. For example, for the before-start checklist phase, as F/O, I had input on the flight recorder panel information such as the service number (that is, WT 251), the trip date (31.01.81) and a digit that signified whether it was the airplane's first trip of the day or not. On the instruments panel are inputs such as the magnetic course for the trip. In this case, for Enugu, I inserted a magnetic course of 100 degrees on the Horizontal Situation Instrument (HSI) course window for steering reference when finally airborne. The

HSI has a compass superimposed on it. Primarily, this instrument depicts the airplane's position with respect to the manual switching made by the pilot to suit the phase of flight at that point in time. For our departure phase, the right switching is the VOR which means Very high frequency Omni-directional Range (and not Velocity of Rotation as published in one of the widely read dailies in the country). The HSI has a bug reference that the pilot manually manipulates to depict the heading he intends to maintain in reference to the fixed compass lubber line. When the heading bug and the compass lubber line are synchronised, then the airplane is on the chosen straight path. I placed the heading bug on 186, which was the magnetic heading for runway 19L, our departure runway. The next input was on the altitude alert panel. This panel is used for the purpose of reminding the pilot of his target altitude as per the clearance from the ATC unit any time the right altitude is set. For the phase of my flight (before start engine), I dialled an altitude figure of the customary 10,000 ft. I continued to the navigational/communication panel where I turned on the Automatic Direction Finding instrument (ADF), by leaving the switch in box position that had ADF written on it. Also on the box, I dialled the departure frequency 336 as published. The ADF is a navigational facility and also a landing facility. The one I selected was installed on the ground somewhere around Agege motor road. It was unfortunately stolen in 1990, and the robbers, in the process of their madness, killed the guard/operator of this facility as reported by one of the Nigerian dailies then. The identifier Morse code of the facility is LA. Pilots generally refer to it as Lima Alpha. This reference is absolutely an aviation term. Digressing a little, the theft of the Lima Alpha was a very sad loss to pilots. In my career experience, before it got stolen by virtue of its location it had really aided pilots during low-level manoeuvres in very poor visibility around Lagos during the landing phase, and had really saved a lot of people (pilots generally) from disaster. The heinous crime these pilferers committed cannot be quantified in years of jail sentence. I pray that these people (whoever they are) know the gravity of their acts so that the guilt of their knowledge shall continue to hunt them. This facility to pilots was a big gateway to runway 19L in poor weather conditions. The absence of it has made poor weather manoeuvres on the left runway in Lagos during landing a "toss-up" situation.

Leaving the ADF boxes, I now turned on the Lagos VOR facility by first of all turning the component selector switch to the Distance Measuring Equipment position, and then dialling in 113.7 MHz into the navigation frequency indicator through the frequency selector switch. I then flipped the audio switch on to confirm the right tuning by listening for the Morse code LG. This is the Lagos VOR facility that pilots refer to as Lima Golf. Lastly, I synchronised my clock on the instrument panel with the BBC time.

It was after all this switching, tuning and identifying had been completed that we finally completed the before-start checklist by calling the checklist complete as required by law. The captain, now following a flow panel pattern by recall, accomplished the cleared to start actions and then called for the cleared to start checklist.

Basically, in starting most aircraft engine the provisos are: (1) a starter unit; (2) electrical energy; (3) air; (4) igniters. All these, and of course fuel, should lead to a normal start with the crystallisation of all these conditions. As soon as we completed reading the checklist, the captain now looked out for the ground monitoring engineer, who had two fingers raised already because part of the cleared to start checklist leads the captain to switch on the anti-collision light, which on ground signifies the readiness of the crew, vis-à-vis engine start. The captain reciprocated the two-finger action which signified that engine number two was being started. During engine start, pilots perform their different roles in achieving a successful and hitch-free start. The captain, by law, is solely responsible for this task, while the co-pilot aids him by making some very vital and mandatory standard call-outs. As soon as the captain commenced the start sequence and things got going, I called out to the captain, "Oil pressure is rising." This he acknowledged by saying, "Roger," which means "I heard you". While I made that call-out, the captain's eyes were darting around as expected, all over the engine instruments. I made my last call of starter cut out, and as expected of him he checked for the increase in pressure on the duct pressure gauge which confirmed the starter cut out, and simultaneously he announced that the exhaust gas temperature (EGT) had stabilised, which betokened a successful start. The captain now raised one finger to inform the ground engineer of his readiness in starting the number one engine. The engineer will only reciprocate this one-finger action when he is completely assured that the engine area is safe and the fireman is in place.

Well, starting number one engine was a matter of repeating the last start sequence. On completion of this I now announced the checklist complete. Meanwhile, while we were busy in the cockpit, things were also happening in the cabin. But for now all we needed to know from the cabin staff was the passenger number on board, and since we had our engines running the cabin staff had to inform us that all passengers were seated and well strapped-in. In response to this information, my duty as co-pilot, was to now furnish the cabin hand with information including (1) destination field, that is, Enugu; (2) cruising altitude/flight time; and also to remind him once again of the captain's name, all of which I did. At this point, the captain ordered door closure. Without waiting for him to prompt me, I requested for taxi clearance from the ATC unit in Lagos.

Once again, dialogue with Lagos tower ensued.

WT 251: "Lagos tower, WT 251 position local ramp, ready to taxi. Destination, Enugu."

Lagos tower: "Roger 251, cleared taxi runway 19L. Call me at the holding point. Souls on board and endurance? QNH now 1013 millibars. Temperature: 33 degrees Celsius."

WT 251: "Cleared taxi, call you holding point, 19L, 1013, 33 degrees Celsius. Souls on board 29, endurance 3 hours. Standing by for departure clearance."

Lagos tower: "Roger 51, stand by for clearance."

In the meantime, the captain, after ground clearance from the ground personnel to leave the ramp, had checked with me if my side of the airplane was clear of obstructions, while I was busy requesting taxi clearance. I just looked out and nodded back to him in the affirmative. He then advanced the throttles of the airplane, put on the taxi light, called out to me to select 16½ flap position which I set for him by moving the flap lever from 0 position to 16½ and then in a commanding tone he requested for the taxi-before-take-off checklist. Now, before I go on, let us quickly look into these words: throttle; flaps; taxi.

The throttles of most airplanes are lever-type structures that are placed and arranged in such a way that their manipulation is only effectively possible by hand motion. The opening and closing of these levers (i.e. advancing and reducing) increases and decreases thrust from the engine respectively. Secondly, the component called flap is a dual-purpose component depending on the selected position. The component or the surface is an integral part of the airplane's wing structure. It is an aerodynamic surface that enhances lift during take-off and also can be positioned in such a way that it will turn to a drag-inducing surface. This latter position is only desirable when there is need to slow down the airplane speed, most often during the landing phase of a flight. Taxi is the movement of aircraft on the ground. This is the only phase of airplane operation when one may logically say that the ticket fare is a combination of a usual cab fare on ground and the air fare when the airplane finally gets airborne.

We left the ramp and made a right turn to get on the taxi way for runway 19L as soon as we were established on the taxi path by reference to the yellow line. I started reading the taxi-before-take-off checklist as commanded by the captain. While reading the checklist we taxied past the company's airplanes hangar. The hangar is the maintenance garage-like structure area where major faults of an airplane are rectified. It is the airplane's clinic or hospital. We passed the hangar to the right or starboard of the airplane. We then passed to the starboard as we continued along the general aviation section of the airport's local wing, which had a museum of antique airplanes, such as the DC3, DC6, the French Caravelle, and so on. The Caravelle, as an airplane, has in her cabin the unique arrangement of passengers seating face to face and looking at each other. Up to today, I still can't figure out the rationale behind this arrangement except for a situation where the passenger facing you by luck happens to be an ornamental-type damsel; then one may have a field day, feasting one's eye on her physical statistics. Conversely too, I imagined what it would be like, if the passengers in the cabin were members of those two major rival political parties in 1981, i.e. UPN, and the ruling party, NPN. I feel their seating face to face to each other would be a foregone conclusion of a disastrous flight. Remember, it was politics with consummate bitterness then, until the military got them sorted out.

Well, the airplane was moving towards the holding point of runway 19L, and the taxi checklist also had got to the item that says crew briefing. The captain then told me I would be doing the flying to Enugu. In that case I had to do the take-off briefing. Crew briefing is something pilots do every day when actively engaged in flight execution. So in short, it becomes a routine habit or custom. The concept behind this procedure is for the pilot flying (PF) to state clearly all his actions and intentions in carrying out the prescribed procedure for the next phase of flight or task he is about to perform. The format as per Take/Off (T/O) briefing goes thus:

> "This would be a right hand seat departure, flaps 16½, runway 19L. Please monitor all engine instruments, and call out any malfunction affecting safety. Set T/O power before 60 kts, call 80 kts for speed cross-check, the V speeds are as stated (on the bug card). If there is any malfunction affecting safety of flight before V1, the captain shall call stop and abort the T/O, in case the malfunction is an engine failure, then our acceleration height in Lagos, would be 0900 ft, the present QNH is 1013. [While I was going through the sing song, the captain had already copied our departure clearance from Lagos tower.] Our departure clearance was WT 251, cleared to the Lagos Upper Terminal area, en route Enugu, and to maintain flight level 170, and after departure, to turn left on course."

All this information was read back to Lagos tower as required by law. All clearances from an ATC unit to an airplane station must be read back so as to avoid any doubt. Before I go on, let us look into certain words or phrases that may not seem to be self-explanatory. Take, for example, in my departure crew briefing speech, I mentioned that the T/O would be aborted if any serious malfunction occurred before the airplane accelerated to the V1 speed. Generally speaking airplane manufacturers utilise different colours of light to first of all indicate to the pilot that something is happening to a component, then the gravity of the malfunction can easily be interpreted by the crew, by virtue of their training. The different colours used are amber, red and blue. An amber light is a caution light that warns the pilot of an impending malfunction, and if disregarded may lead to component damage. The red light is also a warning light that informs the crew that an emergency situation has occurred which needs an immediate action, neglect of which may cause damage to the airplane and subsequent injuries to the occupants. The blue light is an advisory light, meaning the crew have the option of dealing with the situation when time permits. So to abort or reject On/Off, and prior to V1 too, engine failure, engine fire, unsafe configuration, or any adverse condition significantly affecting the safety of flight, are the valid conditions that would attract this manoeuvre. Probing further into the last and rather ambiguous reason, in my career I have had to abort T/O once at Yola airport (in the north eastern part of Nigeria), due to dogs and goats crossing the runway; in Lagos due to a mad man walking across the runway; and in Conakry, Guinea, due to dogs sitting on the runway, coupled with some youngsters playing soccer on the runway too.

It is assumed that at all times the rejected T/O manoeuvre is the captain's responsibility. We were now at the holding point area of runway 19L, waiting for T/O clearance. One of the two cabin staff came into the cockpit and announced to us that the cabin was set for T/O. Without this confirmation from the cabin it would be very unsafe and unairmanlike to start a take-off roll, because if for any reason a passenger is not strapped in, and after take-off we unfortunately run into low-level turbulence, it may cause grave injury to the passenger. Though the passenger's action itself is contributory negligence per se, the cabin announcement would have obviated this. Also, for me at the holding point, I started getting that butterfly-in-the-stomach feeling usually referred to as "checkitis". Pilots only feel this way when they are under some form of check or other. Before the unwelcome feeling could metastasise through my alimentary canal only to gaseously exit my anus, causing a very lousy odour of a fart, I heard my captain reading back to Lagos tower that we had been cleared for T/O with a left turn out and to contact Lagos approach (centre) on VHF frequency 124.3 MHz. The captain then gave a command for the cleared T/O checklist to be read, which I did while he was simultaneously lining up the airplane on the runway for take-off. I then announced the checklist complete and as he was fully lined up I told him the approach path was clear as far as the eye could see. Right there, Captain Valerio took his hands off the throttle levers and said, "It's all yours now, Ty, take me to Enugu." As I advanced the throttles, my checkitis got worse. In effect, the fart odour got more concentrated too. I opened the throttles to the 90 degrees position, and when the captain called out that the engine RPM (rotations per minute) were synchronised, I opened the throttle further, and called out to the captain to set take-off thrust. That he did, and told Lagos tower that WT 251 was rolling, and the tower replied, "Roger, 251." As we continued the take-off run, the take-off fart now started reducing; the captain then called out 80 kts (as per my briefs) and I responded by saying cross-checked. I still kept my hands in position, the left one on the throttle lever, and my right hand on the control stick. The captain then called out that all instruments were in the green arc, which meant so far the take-off was in order. As soon as he called out "*Rotate*" I checked my airspeed indicator for rotation speed confirmation, now removed my left hand from the throttle and placed it on the control wheel and simultaneously, and meticulously too, for passenger comfort, gradually pulled back on the control stick, and anon we were airborne.

Since the captain was the PNF, and I was the PF, he then took over the role and some duties performed by procedure as a first officer. That is to say he was solely in charge of the two-way communication with the different Air Traffic Service units (ATS units) throughout the flight duration. So getting airborne, the captain called to me "Positive rate of climb" with reference to the Instantaneous Vertical Speed Indicator (IVSI) gauge that had the needle pointer pointing above zero, which relatively showed the airplane was in a climb. I responded to his call out by requesting in a polite but positive command tone with the phrase "Gear up please," and at about 500 ft above Lagos elevation I started initiating a turn to the left to get established on course to Enugu. At 800 ft above the ground, I called for flap retraction to the zero position and for trimmers and climb power, and I kept on climbing and accelerating at the same time towards my target flight level (FL) of 170, and my target climb speed of 165 kts with the throttle setting at climb power setting too. The captain signed off from the Lagos tower frequency and changed to the Lagos approach frequency of 124.3 MHz.

To establish contact with a new ATS unit under the same jurisdiction, all you have to do is transmit. Since the last ATS unit has already informed the next unit about your presence, the dialogue is even simpler. While the captain was busy trying to establish contact with Lagos approach, I checked the flap lever at zero with a zero reading on the flap gauge itself, and then I called out for the after-take-off checklist. This is the only checklist procedure in almost all commercial airplanes where the crew member going through this checklist does so silently, and on completion he just calls out: "After-take-off checklist complete." To establish contact with Lagos approach the dialogue now was:

WT 251: "Lagos approach, good afternoon. This is WT 251."

Lagos approach: "WT 251, good afternoon, this is Lagos approach, go ahead."

WT 251: "Roger WT 251 with you in a left turn, out of 2,500 ft for FL 170. Call you back for estimates."

Lagos Approach: "Roger 251, cleared on course, give your estimates when ready, and call me passing FL 100, for 170."

WT251: "Lagos approach, WT 251, estimates Lagos UTA at 1335Z, and Enugu destination at 1425Z, presently out of 110 for 170, and established on course."

Lagos tower: "WT 251, estimates copied, call me UTA, and maintaining FL 170."

WT 251: "Will do, Lagos tower."

Meanwhile, we were supposed to change our altimeter setting at Lagos transition altitude of 3,500 ft to the standard setting of 1013 mb which luckily was our QNH in Lagos during take-off.

This standard setting is called QNE, of which transition altitude or level as the case may be differs from one station to another. So at the time I climbed through 3,500 ft we both said in chorus, "1013 mb set." Climbing through FL 100, I called for passing FL 100 actions, which for the PNF was to turn off the inboard landing light that had been on since take-off and also put the "No Smoking & Fasten Seat-Belt" switch to the Auto-Off position. At this point too, I engaged the autopilot. I went ahead and completed my paperwork by filling the Voyage Report booklet with entries such as service number, date of service, crew nomenclature, airplane take-off weight, fuel on board during start, origin of service engine start up time, passenger number etc. A space of a few lines was left for the captain to make whatever comments about the service that may have been of importance to the company. If none, he just enters "Nil" in the remarks column. Then I picked up the tech-log to enter the service number, and, this time only, cockpit crew nomenclature in order of rank, date of flight, and the take-off time out of Lagos.

Since the flipping of the fasten seat belt switch to the off position in the cockpit means "uhuru" in the cabin, as soon as that light went off in the cabin, the cabin staff came to the cockpit to inquire about our individual needs as far as meals were concerned. As for me, my meal was the check flight, so I made no request for any menu; only the captain and his bona fide F/O requested meals. I must point out here, once and for all, the crew meal concept adopted by almost all operating commercial airlines globally. The concept is: it is highly recommended that the captain and the co-pilot should not have the same meal, and in the eventuality where they have no choice, both crew should consume their meals at an interval of at least an hour from each other. The bottom line of this concept is basically safety. It is assumed that in the case of the meal being contaminated, the corollary of which is a food-poisoned crew member, at least one is still intact and assumed okay to successfully complete the flight. Pilots go through the practice of one-man crew operation in flight simulation facilities. So in the event of this happening in real life, there should be no cause for panic.

As soon as we levelled off at FL 170, I picked up the let-down chart for Enugu, and started studying it. As a matter of fact, there are two let-down published procedure charts for the Enugu runway, predicated on two facilities, i.e. the VOR (EU) or simply Echo Uniform, and the ADF (EN) Echo November.

Before I go on into the literature of let-down approach charts, since we were now in the cruise phase of the flight, and Captain Sperry was also doing the flying now, of course, as in most semi-democratic cockpits (because by law, since the captain has been endowed with autocratic power, his authority over his crew members is absolute), with Sperry on duty now (Sperry is the autopilot manufacturer's name), apart from monitoring Mr Sperry, and also with clear skies, for that short or long period, as the case may be, before descending to destination airport, it was now time to entertain each other so to speak. Because I must say, the process of flight execution, due to relatively long years of being involved in it, now gets routine and of course becomes boring, sometimes to an insipid level, especially if unluckily one gets stuck flying with some personalities that you find, in your own opinion, incompatible with you. In a cockpit environment all forms of communication are so formal that I think airplane manufacturers should make a checklist of them apart from the airplane's quick reference checklist. Situations have sometimes led to cockpit frays.

Well, luckily for me, for this particular flight check the cockpit environment was as harmonious as it could be. I was with Captain Valerio whom I had found during my line training to be an intelligent extrovert and also a realist with a rather consummate sense of humour. The humour lay in his accent, and with this same accent he cracked very juicy jokes. His conduct and style of living, including his professional attitude if filmed, would be a successful box office sell-out in Hollywood. I still remember vividly one joke he cracked, when he noticed I was getting too serious about the whole flight check. He said that when he was in the Philippines working as first officer for a small air taxi outfit, he could recall one flight check reminiscent of mine. He said there was this very skilful and brilliant second officer who was on a check that would upgrade him to the F/O position. During the check the chap, as expected, demonstrated such a mastery of the aircraft that instead of his check composition of having to fly to three different destinations in fulfilment of his company's requirements, the overwhelmed check pilot just passed him based on his performance during the first leg of the three-leg trip. So the chap went home satisfied that at last he'd got it made. Since he had passed the check, it was to take precisely a week and a half for the paper of recognition of his new status to be released. The paper was also to confirm that the second officer was now qualified to be rostered as a substantive F/O. Captain Valerio took a look at me and said, "You know what, Ty! The company suddenly shut down four days after the guy's flight check. So tell me, how does that grab you?"

"This can only grab me in one way," I replied.

Then he asked curiously again, "How?"

My reply was so easy and simple. I just said to him, "It grabbed me the way it grabbed the other guy." He and the co-pilot just cracked up because the way I answered the question showed I would not want to be that guy. Thank God the event took place in the Philippines and not in Nigeria, otherwise it would have been too close for comfort.

Cockpit entertainment comes in different forms. One that I recall vividly, and always looked forward to, involved a captain that I flew under as co-pilot on a B737 airplane on fourteen different occasions between the 27th of March 1983 and the 9th of October 1984. On all these occasions the captain proved beyond reasonable doubt that he was a cockpit celebrity. Any time we were flying together and got to a comfortable cruising level, with the seat belt lights off, he began to make things happen. It was the classic case of what's in a name. As a matter of fact, he was a household name. His name rang prosperity all over the country when it was mentioned and signalled the rise of living standards. For me personally, if not for this name I would never have flown an airplane. My parents would never have been able to raise my tuition as a private student pilot if not for this name.

Before we got to cruising altitude, the cockpit was usually filled with all sorts of complimentary cards, handwritten notes, and an ocean of verbal messages for this captain. And once the cruising altitude was reached, the entertainment started with a rather unique problem. The captain normally began to ask questions about the gender, societal status, categorical classification of needs and the hierarchy of the people who came to the cockpit. And it was usually a continuous pilgrimage to the airborne throne of consultation that the cockpit became whenever he was the captain in charge. I must confess that I always enjoyed every bit of that entertainment.

So WT 251 had just reported passing Lagos Upper Terminal Area at time 1333Z, maintaining FL 170, and establishing on the 100 radial of the LG (Lima Golf) VOR. Talking about radials, a VOR facility transmits pulse signals in degrees summing up to 360 degrees, or a full circle (the electrical pulse signal converted to degrees is called radial). The facility is usually located on the ground. Any airplane with an airborne Very High Frequency (VHF) navigational receiver would be able to receive signals from any tuned and operational VOR facility, as long as the airplane was within range of the tuned facility, and there were no obstructions that could cause any form of interference to the signals. For general information, the average range of all the operational VOR facilities in this country is approximately 110 nautical miles. In converting the pulse signals received from the ground facility to magnetic heading, the airplane uses a component called the flux valve, whose primary function is sensing the horizontal component of the earth's magnetic field and converting it to an electronic signal which is displayed as the airplane's magnetic heading on the airplane's Radio Magnetic Indicator (RMI), two of which are installed on the cockpit instrument panel. The airplane's HSI now repeats the magnetic heading displayed on the RMI through the compass system arrangement. Still en route, I was in charge, but in reality Sperry was still actively engaged. At 1333Z, we were now approximately 152 nautical miles from Enugu. Since I was the crew flying then, I had the sole responsibility of doing all the switching as far as navigational aids en route were concerned. I dialled 115.7 MHz with the VOR frequency selector knob, located in front of the area in the cockpit called the pedestal, or the control stand. Then on the ADF box, I dialled 394 Hz EN Non-Directional Beacon (NDB). This aid performs two functions. It may be used as a navigational facility and as a landing aid. The handicap of this aid starts from its name, so to speak. The beacon transmits non-directional signals by which the pilot of an aircraft equipped with direction finding equipment (like ours) could determine his bearing from the radio beacon and home in or track to or from the station. The aid is prone to weather phenomena like thunderstorms and interference from lightning. Then at night the beacons are vulnerable to interference from distant stations. These aids installed almost all over the different airports in Nigeria are sometimes the source of good and bad news. Let us look at it this way. First, the course alignment accuracy of a VOR facility is excellent, being generally plus or minus one degree, whereas for the NDB the accuracy depends on what the pilot can make of the non-directional signals from it. As a matter of fact, during rainstorms, the needle of this airborne instrument would just point to the area of static in the storm's precipitation. Now imagine for example that you are navigating by reference to signals from this facility and en route you have a storm cell almost 110 degrees off your track. The needles of this instrument would just point to the storm cell, so if you are unfortunately unaware of the reason for this erratic change in track and you fall victim to it, i.e. by changing your navigation to 110 degrees off track, then your guess is as good as mine destination-wise.

Now, for some inexplicable reason, these NDB aids are often more in operation than the VOR facility. But I have not heard of any reasonable pilot bringing down his aircraft in a rainstorm with the NDB. If for some reason, you are stuck at a station with only this facility as the let-down aid and the station is in rain, the first thing to bear in mind is that this aid may un-aid you at any time, and when it does it really becomes non-directional. Then the pilot too gets non-directional, as a result of which the airplane naturally joins the non-directional chain. Then if the crew unfortunately gets in a quandary about this surmountable situation, then the only time they would be directional is when they arrive at base in body bags.

In my opinion the NDB should be an aid for insane pilots. As a matter of fact, it is hardly used in the western world any more. I guess they have had a lot of costly experience with the unpredictability of this aid, which totally defeats the scientific concept of a normal let-down procedure that guarantees a positive result as long as it is well executed by the pilot.

While we were still cruising with both landing aids tuned we did not receive signals from EU immediately due to our altitude and range. The EU facility is located with Distance Measuring Equipment (DME). This DME is also pulse-sending equipment except that this time it is a paired pulse with a specific spacing sent from the airplane airborne equipment to the operating ground station tuned. The time lapse in the exchange of signals between the airborne unit and the ground station is translated into the distance (in nautical miles) from the aircraft to the ground station. The accuracy of the DME as long as the principle of line of sight is in order is about 3% of the distance displayed in the DME window. This equipment is very vital to short- and medium-range airplanes, especially the ones without any other distance fix equipment installed such as the Inertia Reference System (IRS), Ground Navigation System (GNS) and sometimes the almost phased-out doppler equipment.

We were now getting closer and closer to Enugu. The captain had tuned into the Enugu control tower frequency of 123.3 MHz, and went ahead to establish contact.

WT 251: "Enugu tower, good afternoon. This is WT 251, over."

Enugu tower: "WT 251, this is Enugu tower; good afternoon, go ahead."

WT 251: "WT 251 is a Fokker 27 from Lagos to Enugu, maintaining FL 170, airborne Lagos at time 1300Z, checked Lagos UTA boundary at 1333Z, and estimates destination Echo-Uniform, at time 1425Z. We have twenty-nine souls on board, and endurance remaining is two hours plus thirty minutes and we request Enugu latest weather report."

Enugu tower: "WT 251, message copied okay, call when ready for descent, Enugu at 1330Z. May I go ahead?"

WT 251: "Roger, go ahead with your weather, over."

Enugu tower: "Enugu at 1330Z, wind: 240/05 kts, CAVOK, temperature: 33 degrees Celsius, QHN: 1013 mb. Runway 27 in use, call when ready for descent."

WT 251: "Roger, weather copied okay, 1013 mb, 33 degrees Celsius, runway 27 in use."

At this point, though I was flying, I pointed out the fact that Enugu tower had given us neither the clearance point nor the type of let-down approach to expect. So on further interrogation about this by the captain to Enugu tower, Enugu responded with: "WT 251, you are cleared to the ED VOR, maintaining FL 170, and expect VOR approach for runway 27, call when ready for descent."

"That's better," I said to the captain. He nodded his head. At this point, I started studying Mr Jeppesen's VOR chart for Enugu runway 27. Now before I continue, let us consider the meaning of the acronym CAVOK. It is simply a meteorological term which means Ceiling And Visibility OKay for the station. A pilot having got this information knows immediately that the station's visibility is 10 km or more; that there are no clouds below 1,500 metres or 5,000 ft, and that the station is in no form of precipitation or thunderstorm. Also, I should quickly point out here that for most runways landing can be made from both ends. For example, the Enugu runway has two magnetic take-off and landing directions. That is to say, for the VOR, you have 264 degrees and 084 degrees as magnetic headings usually rounded up to the last digit to depict the runway's designation on the charts. That is to say, in Enugu, for the runway's magnetic direction of 264 degrees, the runway would be referred to as runway 27, and for 084 degrees it would be runway 09. A pilot's choice of the suitable runway to use for a landing or take-off, as the case may be, depends primarily on the prevailing wind direction and speed in relation to the runway magnetic heading. The pilot at all times tries as much as possible to land into the wind with the minimum crosswind effect. The crosswind is that wind vector that acts at a different angle to the airplane's flight path. Sometimes, if this wind vector is acting at an angle of 90 degrees and at a relatively high velocity (30 kts and above) to the airplane's flight path during landing, it may cause an uncontrollable landing path for the airplane and an eventual disaster. So in effect, for the reported wind in Enugu, the most ideal runway for landing as far as the wind information went was runway 27. This though was just one vital determinant, among many others, another of which was the approach procedure chart (published only for runways recognised all over the world as instrument runways). Most of the instrument approach charts in use today are published by Jeppesen & Co, who, after gathering navigational information from very reliable sources concerning a particular station, come up with the display of visual cues about the station in pictorial form, with orthogonal projections for take-off and landing path all reflected or designed in such a way that all experienced and instrument-rated pilots who understand the basic principles and the necessary limitations of the publication would be able to utilise the chart effectively. The publishers believe that all the information in their charts has been edited and is therefore correct. The company also stresses in its publications that since no warranty has been placed on the accuracy of the source materials, their company assumes no responsibility towards a person or persons connected with the use of their chart.

This philosophy of theirs could be traced back to many decades ago when an avid eighteen-year-old private pilot's license holder, known as Jeppesen, took relish in flying around the air space, and, while flying, made a sketch of his flight path. As time went on, research was made into this information and a way was finally found of making it useful. Being able to follow precisely the procedure depicted on these charts is the scientific department in flight execution. So while I was busy rehearsing the details of the VOR let-down chart for Enugu 27, the captain was now in contact with our company's dispatch office in Enugu on frequency 131.5 MHz and had got across to them information like airplane registration, name of captain in command, number of crew on board, estimated regulated take-off weight for the return trip to Lagos, quantity of fuel for the return trip, arrival time in Enugu, and, lastly, request for any ground support equipment needed for the turnaround period on the ground in Enugu. After the captain had signed off with the company's frequency, I now engaged him in the dialogue of the let-down procedure for the VOR approach runway 27 in Enugu. After a few minutes of the let-down literature, the captain just responded by saying, "Ty, make sure you fly what you have just bored me with." He was right about that. Briefing a let-down is one thing, but being able to carry out precisely what the chart says is another ball game. As a matter of fact the instrument let-down forms a major part in the total assessment of a pilot as to what class he belongs in the professional field. Tersely put, the mastery of instrument flying is IT in flight execution. Since during my crew briefing I had indicated to the captain at what point I would appreciate descent into Enugu, and Enugu tower had instructed us to request for descent when ready, the captain obliged me by doing this at 61 miles from the EU VOR. Enugu tower cleared us to FL 50 with the clearance point still RU and also instructed us to call him approaching FL 50 for further descent and to report over the VOR facility. At this point (61 miles) I closed the thrust levers, pushed the airplane control stick forward, and looked at my Instantaneous Vertical Speed Indicator (IVSI) to establish a descent rate of 3,000 ft per minute so as to arrive over Enugu VOR facility at 5,000 ft initially. During descent I now called for the descent and approach checklist. While we are busy reading and responding to the item for that checklist phase, Enugu tower cleared us further to an altitude of 3,500 ft on the local QNH of 1013 mb, and then for the instrument let-down for VOR runway 27, and instructed us to advise him arriving over the facility and commencing the approach.

I must clarify here that with the prevailing weather in Enugu one did not need to go through the onerous task of flying the instrument let-down procedure for runway 27. This is because in flying the pilot is faced with two weather conditions. One is the condition that gives room for visual flight rules, while the other and poorer condition necessitates instrument flight rules. These two conditions are called VFR and LFR conditions respectively. So one can easily gather that the usefulness of an instrument let-down procedure chart is in an LFR condition. So, logically speaking, since the weather report for Enugu was the VFR type I should have requested for a visual let-down for runway 27. Visual let-downs, in nature, are quite easy to accomplish and are less time consuming. But since my flight was a check flight, with an instrument let-down forming part of the check format, weather or no weather, I had to carry out this instrument let-down.

As we descended through FL 100, the captain told me to dis-engage Captain Sperry (the automatic pilot unit), and now fly the

Approach Control through Tower
*ENUGU Tower (R) 123.3 121.7

3500'	2500'

MSA
EU VOR

Alt Set: hPa | Trans level: FL 50 | Apt. Elev 466'
| | Trans alt: 3500' (3085') | |

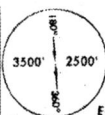

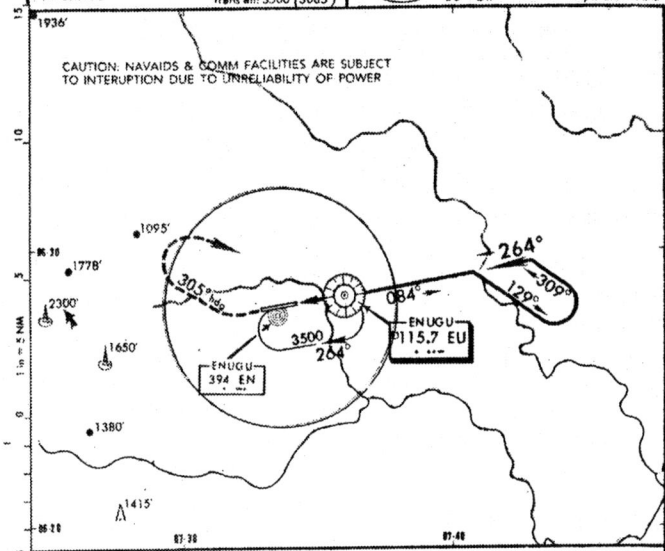

1936'

CAUTION: NAVAIDS & COMM FACILITIES ARE SUBJECT
TO INTERUPTION DUE TO UNRELIABILITY OF POWER

•1095'

96 30
•1778'

⌂2300'

•1650'

305° hdg

264°

3500

264°

—ENUGU—
394 EN

—ENUGU—
115.7 EU

084°

264°

309°

129°

•1380'

Λ1415'

86 28   87 30   87 40

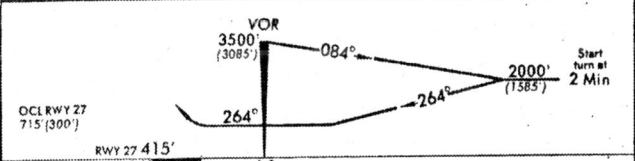

VOR
3500'
(3085')

084°

264°

2000'
(1585')

Start
turn at
2 Min

264°

OCL RWY 27
715' (300')

RWY 27 415'
APT. 466'   0   1.8

MISSED APPROACH: Turn RIGHT climb on heading 305° to 2000' (1585'), then turn
RIGHT and return to VOR climbing to 2500' (2085').

STRAIGHT - IN LANDING RWY 27		
MDA(H) 720' (305')		

		ALS out	
A			
B	1200m	1600m	
C			
D	1600m		

Gnd speed-Kt	70	90	100	120	140	160
VOR to MAP	1.8	1.33	1.12	1.05	0.54	0.46	0.41

CHANGES Minimums.

NOT DRAWN TO SCALE

airplane manually. The check had commenced again. I took Sperry off and used the airplane trim mechanism to trim off any heavy loads from the airplane flight control surfaces to make life easier for me in flying it. As I started to level out at 3,500 ft as cleared by Enugu tower, I was shocked to find that I was hunting all over the place in trying to maintain this altitude steadily. I started cursing under my breath. "I just must not mess this chance up," I kept telling myself. The captain just sat there watching the sweat pattern on my face in that air-conditioned cockpit. I must say that for those who know the ailment that was the first physical symptom of "checkitis". We got over the EU facility and the let-down procedure got under way. The captain continued with the task of communicating with the tower and I with the task of flying the airplane according to the procedure on the chart.

The procedure chart requires that the pilot should fly the airplane in such a way that he must arrive over the EU facility at 3,500 ft + 100 ft, minus 0 ft (as the altitude control limitation), and then do certain things as soon as he leaves the facility. He thumbs the elapsed time switch on the clock located on his instrument panel, since the procedure stipulates a two-minute flying time away from the EU facility. While established on the 084 radial, the prescribed and published procedure was to descend to an altitude of 2,000 ft. In the process of adhering to this procedure, the pilot is also saddled with the responsibility of reducing his speed gradually, in such a way that at completion of the entire let-down procedure, he would simultaneously have attained the optimum landing speed for the airplane, referred to as Vref speed. The Vref speed is the airplane's landing reference speed. It is usually depicted by the pilot manually using the airspeed indicator bugs to set this speed so that at any time during the landing phase he may be able to achieve an easier and a quicker reference to his landing speed, in concert with other information on the instrument panel that he must continue to scan, in a pattern that would make him attain the published result. So a pilot in slowing down the airplane starts to deploy drag-inducing flight control surfaces called flaps to achieve different speeds at different but mandatory schedules. During landing, the first two flap schedules, measured in degree angles, are referred to as intermediate flap settings. These two settings must also be achieved within the two minutes' span of leaving the let-down facility. After a two-minute lapse, maintaining 2,000 ft, you now steer the airplane to the right from the magnetic heading and the VOR radial 084 to a heading of 129 degrees. This heading is what is referred to as the procedure turn heading. It is always a standard 45 degree heading change either right or left of the magnetic course one left of the facility. This magnetic heading, or facility radial, or track, as the case may be, is what is referred to as the outbound procedure course leg. In the case of the VOR let-down in Enugu, the procedure turn was to the right with a 45 degree heading change that gave a resultant heading (084 + 45) of 129 degrees. Also, all turns in a let-down procedure were assumed to have been carried out maintaining a 25 degree bank angle, which is referred to as the standard rate of turn. If adhered to, this guarantees a constant heading change of three degrees per second.

As soon as I established on the 129 degree heading, and still battling hard to hold 2,000 ft altitude as steadily as possible, I timed again on this heading for 45 seconds, after which I made a final course reversal towards the new inbound radial to the runway of 084 degree radial by maintaining an intercept heading of 309 degrees (as published in the chart). An intercept heading is the heading an airplane maintains in order to establish on a desired facility radial or track in the shortest possible time. All through this process, the PNF is also busy in the procedure loop with the PF, making some call-outs as required by law and simultaneously keeping a constant two-way communication with the control tower. The communication basically involves position reports in relation to the prescribed procedure. The moment I established on the 084 radial of EU I requested the extension of the landing gear and three green lights appeared in front of me. The green lights meant the gears were extended and safe for a landing. I then requested the landing checklist while already commencing my final descent towards the runway. Suffice it to mention here that instrument let-downs are categorically bifurcated. The primary let-down is the non-precision category while the secondary one is the more advanced and sophisticated precision category. What makes the difference here is that the non-precision approach is a standard approach in which no electronic glide slope is provided. For the latter (i.e. the precision category) an electronic glide slope is provided. The glide slope equipment also incorporates a ground facility and an airplane is equipped with a receiver. As for the VOR let-down in Enugu, no provision was made for an electronic glide slope, which classified the procedure under the non-precision category.

So at that point, I commenced my final descent towards the runway after being established on the final approach course of 264 degrees, called the final approach fix. Once the landing gear is extended, the next phase of tasks for both the cockpit and cabin crew is set to commence. It is at about this moment that the cabin hand goes into the boring rhetoric of, "In a short while from now," and the rest of the routine.

As for the pilot, he has a final descent altitude, a final descent altitude target, and also a calculated missed approach point in case he feels that the continuation of the approach may lead to an undesirable result. It is this fixed phase of an approach to landing path, predicated either on a fix passage, DME fix or just plain timing, that is called the missed approach or Go Around point. It is mandatory, legally, that if at this point the pilot has not properly established his airplane in a safe landing path, or does not have the runway in sight, he must carry out a missed approach. Or, in common parlance, he must climb back up to try and re-establish a better and more precise landing path.

As a co-pilot, I did quite a few overshoots or missed approaches myself both on the Boeing 737 airplane and later on, on the European Airbus 310. The record breaking experience I had was on the 26th of May, 1983, on the Boeing 737, WT 250/609 routing Lagos–Enugu–Port Harcourt. Port Harcourt was the change-over station for us cockpit crew. Unfortunately, that day Port Harcourt was shrouded in rain showers. The equipment was 5N-ANZ. All in the name of making a landing in Port Harcourt, we recorded a record-breaking feat of four overshoots or missed approaches, with my captain recording three attempts, while I made one attempt and came back to make a final landing. It was this nightmarish experience and others similar to it that led me to form the opinion (as captain) that the first attempt in an instrument let-down procedure, in poor visibility or any other weather condition, is the best attempt. This is purely a personal opinion, and I always make sure that I never carry out a procedure twice except of course as a correctional measure when I have a crew member undergoing line indoctrination training under me. I always tell my co-pilot during let-down briefing that, "*It is only one shot, gentleman, then we get out of here.*" So far, it has worked for me as captain.

So in the process of my controlled descent towards my target minimum descent altitude of 720 ft, for the Enugu runway 27, the captain called out to me as expected that the field was now in sight and straight ahead of me. My response by training was asking for the selection of final landing flaps and calling for the total completion of the landing checklist. As soon as we accomplished this, the captain informed me of our being cleared to land on runway 27 in Enugu. The target minimum descent altitude is usually abbreviated as the MDA or, simply put, this is the lowest altitude expressed in feet above mean sea level to which descent is authorised on final approach in the execution of a standard instrument approach procedure where no electronic glide slope is provided. It was toward this altitude that I was descending when the captain called out that the field was in sight. At this point, I moved from the instrument procedure to a visual path, now using my visual contact with the runway to adjust my final descent and landing profile. I simultaneously reduced to my final landing speed and continued towards the runway. Eventually, I touched down smoothly on runway 27 in Enugu.

As soon as I touched down, the captain in a very clear and positive command tone called out "I have controls." This call out reverts the PF back to the PNF while reverting the captain, who until now was the PNF, to his status as the PF. As soon as he took over, he commenced immediate braking action, both from the foot brakes and aerodynamically from the propeller pitch change, called the ground fine pitch. We stopped and took exit from the runway, before the captain called out for the after-landing checklist. While accomplishing this, I had already taken over the role of communicating with the tower. The after-landing checklist was consulted when the airplane was parked. It was then that I read both the after-landing checklist and the engine-shut-down checklist and announced their completion. This checklist for the crew signifies trip termination until the next one starts. In the cabin, it signifies the expiration of both the passenger ticket coupon and the boarding pass for that trip.

Well, back in the cockpit, we were now parked and subsequently sitting and waiting for support services equipment like the airplane step and the external electrical ground power unit to be provided. I just sat there, frozen and generally rewinding and replaying the tale of the let-down tape. I was also trying as far as possible, to grade my performance.

I remember the song the captain had kept singing during the let-down. "Ty, the book says 2,000 ft and not 2,200 ft; Ty, please do something about this." When correcting he would now go into the Filipino-like tenor, then later on soprano, singing again, "Hey, Ty, take it easy with your pitch change, the passengers have paid for a smooth flight, Ty, so please give it to them, Ty, the airplane is like a lady, Ty, so treat her like one, Ty, and be gentle with her." I still recall that moment vividly in my mind today because I was getting so worked up and sweating so profusely that the moment I heard "treat her like a lady" I just said under my breath, with all annoyance, "Oh yeah? If that's the case, why don't you go f… her you Filipino …hole."

Since the time we read the shut-down checklist, the captain totally ignored my presence in that cockpit, and completely kept me incommunicado. For me it was a very cruel experience because the successful outcome of this flight check for me meant a lot. And since we had got the first phase of the trip behind us, I logically expected an immediate assessment briefing, especially as I had given myself a marginal pass. Confirmation of this would do a lot in enhancing my performance (without need for steroids) on the next trip. But there I was, all left alone with my sweat-ridden black face. That made me even madder, because I sure looked like the guys from the cave days with sweat on my black face. In short, for most people seeing me for the first time in their lives, looking like this, the first word that would probably cross their minds would be *ugly*. This was the same face that my captain glanced at once, smiled and continued with the turnaround departure trip formality with the ground personnel in Enugu.

Talking about trip turnarounds, different air carriers all over the world know fully well, that the time factor is a vital vehicle to profit earnings, and therefore the importance of time in all facets of an airline's operation cannot be overemphasised. In the case of an airplane's turnaround duration, factors considered include airplane size (vis-à-vis passenger capacity), station manpower and the assumption that individual members of all units involved in this operation are well versed in their roles and understand the aims and objectives of the whole exercise. The responsibility of the cockpit crew members during turnaround begins the moment the airplane approaches the particular station, because by procedure the pilot would have made contact with his company's dispatch office at the station and passed all the information earlier discussed to the ground personnel in the hope of achieving full ground readiness as soon as the airplane lands and disembarks the passengers on board. The turnaround process involves the captain functioning as captain and supervisor, on the ground and in the air. And for the captain to be effective and efficient as a supervisor, he must not only be adept in his own professional field but must have, to a relatively acceptable degree, a liking for people, emotional stability, integrity, courage and fortitude, enthusiasm for his work, and a high ethical standard.

With all these qualities, the captain as a supervisor is bound to relish his role. With all hands on deck, the company's stipulated turnaround time for Enugu station (based on the aforementioned provisos) is thirty minutes. Apart from the cockpit task, the other tasks performed by cockpit crew members during transit are making a general external check of the airplane status and making sure the airplane is still intact for operation. While the pilot is engaged with his own task, other formalities like getting the cabin clean and in suitable condition for the embarking passengers and refuelling the airplane for the next service are simultaneously carried out. If the captain is satisfied that the airplane and crew are ready for the next trip, he now contacts the dispatch office to announce commencement of passenger boarding.

That hot afternoon, I went down as part of my duties to monitor the fuelling of the airplane and also carry out the usual test for fuel contamination before I authorised the refuelling process. These form part of the external tasks of the F/O, my office in view. Walking around the airplane in accomplishing the external checks still didn't defrost me. Back inside the cockpit, I sat down again and robotically went about the return trip cockpit set-up and preparation. Preparing for another take-off is the same routine we had followed in Lagos, the only difference being that we were now taking off from Enugu. So, procedure-wise, it was the same ball game with only a few navigational changes, such as course reversal for Lagos and altitude change, now in even figures following the semi-circular rule, that ensures positive separation from inbound and outbound traffic from a station, with the chosen altitude predicated on the airplane's magnetic course or heading. Then, of course, facility change when in the vicinity of Lagos. As we lined up for another take-off from Enugu runway 27, the captain told me once again to do the flying to Lagos.

It was about three miles from touchdown in Lagos that the captain finally said, "Hey, Ty, I got your papers signed already, congratulations." I went on and landed the airplane, and the captain got her parked. We read the engine-shut-down and parking checklists. Thank God it was all over, and I had made it. My prayer was then for the company not to fold up in the next five days.

Now that's what happens in a day's job. But one question I usually ask is: "When does a flight really terminate?" A contemporary F/O would say it is when the parking checklist has been completed, with all trip documentation finalised, including entries in the airplane's technical log if any, and rounding off the voyage report entries with the captain endorsing it, then walking up to the dispatch office to submit the papers, and finally saying goodbye to everybody. Before I give a philosophical and personal answer to this question, I must emphasise the fact that sometimes in a day's job one might do a five-leg trip. Now, as for when a flight really terminates, I remember that during one of my trips to the British Caledonian facility for the half-yearly mandatory recurrent proficiency check in Gatwick, United Kingdom, my captain and I engaged the simulator instructor and some of his friends on their view about this question. Well, the instructor said that as far as he was concerned, a flight terminated when he had walked one-hundred metres away from the parked airplane. His explanation was simple and practical: he reckoned that were the airplane to explode for some reason, one-hundred metres was quite a safe distance from the explosion. Later on and before we left Gatwick, we found out that the guy lived just one-hundred metres from the airport. For most colleagues I have asked this question *home* seemed to be the general terminating point. Well, it was like this for me for a long time until the Lockerbie incident where some flight crew on their way home got hit and injured from the debris dispersed during the airplane's explosion. Since then I've gone the Japanese way: A *flight has fully terminated when you have successfully reported for your next rostered flight.*

Things usually happen to me in my professional field mostly in the month of January. For instance, I got started in aviation on the 21st of January, 1977. I was also released as a substantive F/O on the F27 airplane in January. My papers to operate from the administrative personnel came out two weeks later, reflecting a pay increase from N5,800 to N8,900. It took from September, 1979 to the 31st of January 1981 to achieve a N3,l00 pay increase.

After I received my paper to operate, my subsequent flights on the F27 became quite uneventful, until a few days to the ides of March, 1981 (06-03-81) when I was operating an extra flight to Enugu, WT 863. The cockpit's composition had me as the legal co-pilot, with the captain and a second officer on line indoctrination training on board. He (the second officer) was occupying my seat and I was on the observer's seat. The day started with beautiful weather and the service left base (Lagos) on schedule, and started climbing as cleared by the Air Traffic Control to FL 230.

As we continued our climb towards our target altitude of 23,000 ft, I started feeling uneasy in my ears as we passed 11,000 ft. I asked the captain what he felt. I had not come on board with any feverish symptoms like catarrh, so this unusual ear pain was certainly not *aerotitis*. Immediately we got to FL 230, the whole thing got worse, and of course the pilot's first guess was a faulty pressurisation system. Well, let's talk about the pressurisation system, and its function as an airplane system or unit. Starting with the background information first, man is essentially an earthling. From authentic medical research, man can survive at sea level without oxygen for eight minutes, but with altitude the air gets thinner, and subsequently the length of time he can survive without oxygen diminishes.

Most air carriers know that in the airline business fuel efficiency, i.e. fuel management, is a major factor in the overall profit-making process of the carrier itself. To achieve this, the airline, as much as possible, goes for the most fuel-efficient airplanes that suit the type of operation the carrier is involved in. But, incidentally, most engines achieve optimum fuel efficiency only at altitudes above FL 230. On the other hand 80% of air carriers' clientele would be earthlings who medically suffer from hypoxia at altitudes above 8,000 ft (hypoxia is simply a deficiency of oxygen in the blood). If most air carriers had to operate at this low altitude with their vast and expensive equipment, then they might as well be flying for the Red Cross International for all the profit they would make. That is, they would make no profit at all.

Well, it didn't take long before the carrier man problem got sorted out. After further technological research, the airplane manufacturers came up with a pressure-regulating unit called the pressure controller. This unit, in conjunction with other components arranged and built along with it, came to be known in high altitude airplanes as the pressurisation system. The system operates in such a way that it maintains, through the pressure controller, a proportional relationship between the ambient (i.e. outside pressure) and cabin pressure. The pressure controller measures or senses pounds per square inch of pressure (psi) and converts it to equivalents in terms of altitude approximately. The controller pressurises the airplane to 125 psi or 200 ft on the ground, and after take-off, regardless of the airplane's actual rate of climb, the controller climbs the airplane's cabin altitude at a proportional rate to the airplane climb rate, to attain a preset and comfortable cabin altitude for the airplane flight altitude. For example, for an airplane at FL 230 cruising altitude, the controller maintains an artificial altitude of 2,480 ft in the cabin. The controller operates in such a way that the airplane's artificial cabin never exceeds 8,000 ft. This way, the airplane manufacturers finally made it possible for the air carriers to fly their planes at fuel-efficient high altitude and make their due profit without any of their clientele suffering from hypoxia.

But the pressure controller as a piece of equipment or a technically functioning unit is prone to failure too. When the unit fails, the tendency naturally is for the airplane cabin altitude, which all along had been fooled by the controller unit to stabilise at artificial cabin altitudes of 8,000 ft and below, to now climb and try to catch up with the real airplane altitude, in our case 23,000 ft. If it does, then it is "home sweet home" for everybody, due to oxygen starvation. The failure of the controller's fool's mate can be disastrous indeed if not quickly arrested. So on service WT 863 on the 6th of March, 1981, the pressure controller fool's mate failed. The controller's failure is usually indicated by the cabin-rate-of-climb indicator showing an abnormal climb of about 2,000 ft per minute and trying very hard to obey the laws of nature, by equalising with the airplane altitude. As soon as I noticed this situation, I drew the attention of the captain to it. His first reaction was to get the second officer out of my seat and I then took over before the captain went into the recall action of emergency descent which happens to be the recommended procedure in this type of emergency situation. While the captain was going through his recall actions, I did my recall items too. During emergency descent manoeuvre, the F/O's role (since the press panel is on his side) after donning his oxygen mask and establishing a two-way communication with the captain on oxygen and boom mike box, is to try to arrest the cabin rate by either using the standby mode or the manual mode of the pressurisation system. If after all these actions the cabin continues to climb, then the captain who had been monitoring the whole process now initiates an emergency descent. So the captain pushed the control stick forward and established a 6,000 ft per minute dive. I dialled 14,000 ft in the altitude alert window, informed Enugu tower that we were in an emergency descent and made a request for FL 140, due to pressurisation malfunction. Enugu wasted no time in clearing us further down to FL 60. The captain while diving down towards Enugu had already, through the passenger address system, informed the passengers about the problem we were encountering and the reason behind the mandatory manoeuvre. He didn't need to talk too much because, as a safety device, once an airplane cabin altitude exceeds 10,000 ft an intermittent horn continues to sound in the cockpit until silenced by the crew. Then, if the cabin gradually climbs above 14,000 ft, oxygen masks would from all passenger service units (PSU) in the cabin, to supply passengers with a continuous flow of oxygen until the airplane reaches a safe altitude. The pilot must also carry out his descent in such a way that he arrives at a safe altitude in a mandatory time of four minutes from the time he commenced his descent.

During our descent to 6,000 ft as cleared by Enugu tower, the captain called for the rapid-depressurisation-emergency-descent checklist. This I read to him, and called the checklist complete afterwards. From there on, we flew at FL 60 all the way to Enugu. It is good to mention here that once an airplane is depressurised the airplane altitude and the cabin altitude maintain the same value. Well, we had got over the problem with no injuries to any passenger, and we eventually landed safely in Enugu. On the ground at Enugu, the captain and I decided to probe further into the probable cause of the unit's malfunction. Our subsequent discovery was that the red pressurisation lever which is used by engineers during maintenance had been left in the *test* position, instead of *normal*. As soon as we placed the handle back to the normal position, the unit started functioning OK again. We eventually embarked the passengers for Lagos, and this time around the flight was uneventful. For the crew in the cockpit, we had learnt a big lesson. That we did not discover this lever in the test position during our pre-flight checkout of Lagos was inexcusable, and, to say the least, it was a good example of "crassa-negligencia". I learnt one thing though: all my pre-flight checks from that day onwards would be carried out meticulously and without any hurry. Apart from this event I had no other abnormal situation occurring during the rest of my career as co-pilot on the F27 fleet. My last flight on this airplane was on the 19th of January, 1981, before I moved on to fly the *jets*.

Boeing my Way

What is Boeing? Well, it is the name of an airplane built by the Boeing Commercial Airplane Company based in Seattle, Washington, USA. The company itself was established by a man known as Mr Boeing. I guess the guy's lucky number must have been seven because his company built almost all commercial jetliners flying today with the number seven appearing twice to indicate the particular Boeing airplane. The company's roll-call of the sevens, included the B707, B727, B737, B747, B757, B767, then while the commercial aviation world was logically waiting for the advent of a 777, the Boeing company spoilt the fun by inserting the letter J in place of the expected number seven, thereby breaking an apparent tradition. So far, the 7J7 has not got airborne.

Well, not to worry, the riddle may be looked at this way for the sake of finding some sort of *solatium* in this disappointment: the letter "J" itself, is an inverted but bent number seven. So far, the advent of either the B7J7 or 777 is a toss-up. Boeing's decision on which of the airplanes may eventually be built depends on the type that attracts the highest number of orders from customers. So far, the B777 seems to have an edge since the B777 had already been test flown on the 12th of June, 1994 and had also got a firm or launch customer for delivery in United Airlines Ltd for May 1995. The "Boeing my way" was the B737-200 series. It is one of the most successful Boeing twin-jet airplanes and had its first flight as 737-100 in April 1967. The German Lufthansa airline was the launch customer in the month of December that same year. Nigeria Airways joined the customer chain in the mid 1970s, owning and later selling Boeing airplanes like the B737, B727, B707 and the prestigious jumbo B747 that made history with the name "spirit of courage".

I had always looked forward to joining the jet club. As a matter of fact, it was one of the major reasons for my joining Nigeria

Boeing 737 Airplane

Airways, which then had a vast variety of jet airplanes. The F27 fleet was shut down completely and some of the airplanes were given to the Nigerian Air Force as the airline opted for the jet age. Its most basic fleet then included the F28 and B737. Even at that time, plans were under way to phase out the F28 as well. The company was streamlining the composition of its airplane fleet to the Boeing/McDonnel Douglas airplanes only. In view of this, the airline had placed orders for five B737-200s in advance, in addition to the two it already had.

Since planning ahead means preparation for action, it was necessary to increase manpower to ensure efficient fleet operation on taking delivery of the additional airplanes. In cognisance of this, six of us were slated for a B737 transition course with four other senior first officers moving to the captain position. We went to United Airlines Ltd, Denver, Colorado, USA in August 1981. The F27 fleet was shut down in June 1981, so we had two months of waiting before proceeding to the transition course. This transition has nothing to do with those transition publications in Nigerian newspapers in respect of departed souls, with some spooky information like "The deceased is survived by Reverend Raba Rhoumy (deceased), Airman Lanni Rhoumy (Ph.D.) UK, Mr Talinkwo Rhoumy (deceased)". And at the foot of the publication one could see something like, "Alhaji Josun Rhoumy (hospitalised), for the family". This form of transition publication is one phenomenon I have never comprehended. The long deceased surviving the newly deceased!

In our own case, we were alive, but only moving up from one airplane to another completely different one. I don't know where this "transition" thing evolved from. In the USA this so-called transition training is called "upgradement training". The two-month waiting period before the scheduled commencement date for the course was two months of telling tales about flying the jet airplane. Most of the tale-telling of course came from pilots already rated on jet airplanes. The tales were quite bizarre, to say the least. Almost 96% of the stories were negative and discouraging pronouncements. The bottom line, simply put, was that we had quite an uphill task ahead of us. To a large extent, I wouldn't blame these tale bearers because, unlike the training programme we went through to obtain our type-rating endorsement on the F27 turboprop airplane where the entire training programme was done on the real airplane itself, jet airplanes are more advanced and sophisticated both in training, and in the successful handling of the airplane itself, i.e. the airplane is high tech, high speed, and has complex and more advanced systems. Since in these modern days anything high tech is also very expensive, to save time and money a contemporary type-rating programme for most commercial jets is a three-phase training programme, excluding the airplane ground school phase. The phases of training (excluding the systems ground school) are the cockpit procedure trainer (CPT), the flight simulator and, lastly, the airplane flight training itself. In the days after the First World War, airplane accidents were so commonplace that devices teaching pilots the basic rules of handling were soon introduced. This involved using merely cut down airplanes in which the structure's controls displacement resulted in crude movement of the machine. Nevertheless, this crude form of flight simulation helped save a few lives.

It was the advent of the Second World War that placed new demands on training devices to accommodate a larger population of pilots having to be quickly acquainted with the feel of the airplane before flying in the real thing. Luckily, the crude state of flight simulation was further improved upon by Mr Ed Link. The Ed Link flight simulator equipment was so successful that airline carriers adopted the equipment as a major facility in the training programme for crew. The bottom line of flight simulation is for the simulator facility to create, as much as possible, an atmosphere of reality, vis-à-vis the total characteristics of the particular airplane in question. The Ed Link equipment was able to achieve a reasonable amount of realism. Over one thousand sales of it between the 1930s and the late 1950s is a good proof of the efficacy of the equipment. Flight simulation has improved further since the digital computer breakthrough of the late 1950s which not only brought training costs down, but also increased the measure of realism. One can draw an inference from an incident at the civil aviation school in Zaria. It involved one of the school's top and long-serving administrative officers, who by virtue of his status had always been invited by Nigerian Airways captains (who were mainly old students of the school) to enjoy the hospitality of flying in the cockpit during normal schedule services. He had got so much of this experience that, whenever he travelled Nigeria Airways, sitting in the cockpit became a norm for him. This was especially so of the F28 jet airplane, which did the higher percentage of flights from Kaduna, the gentleman's boarding point any time he had to go to Lagos. So, after the F28 simulator had been installed in the Zaria school, a curious simulator instructor decided to seek some neutral views about the level of reality which the Zaria simulator facility had. The instructor eagerly prayed hard for the day he would be able to simulate a passenger service to someone who, though quite conversant with the F28 airplane, was oblivious of the technology of flight simulation and of course was not a pilot. Such a person was expected to be able to add two and two together, to figure out the gimmick. The simulator instructor finally found a God-sent candidate in the administrative officer.

It happened in this fashion. The administrative officer had earlier on intimated to the instructor about his plan to travel to Lagos on a particular day, adding that unfortunately, he hadn't been able to purchase his ticket in time, a development which he said would cause a colossal setback to his itinerary which was of great importance to him. Well, the instructor quickly came to his rescue by offering him the cockpit seat in a Nigeria Airways F28 airplane coming over to Zaria on a special flight, bringing some important dignitaries for a scheduled aviation conference in the school. He also told his friend that the airplane would be arriving and going back to Lagos that very evening. So it was his good luck that the airplane was coming. Later in the night, the instructor drove to his friend's house and picked him up for the supposedly special flight. As soon as they got back to the school premises under the blissful cover of darkness, the instructor led the friend to the simulator facility. Of course the equipment was a facsimile of the F28 cockpit which the administrative officer was quite familiar with. Seated in there were two pilots, already well-dressed in Nigeria Airways pilots' uniforms. As soon as the gentleman settled down properly, the instructor put in motion everything involved in a normal flight service from Zaria to Lagos in terms of communication and navigation. The pilots got clearance from Zaria tower to taxi for take-off and were also cleared directly from Zaria to Lagos at FL 260, to establish radio contract with Kano and Kaduna immediately after take-off. Before the simulator instructor bade his friend farewell, he made sure he had present all necessary inputs and information needed for a Zaria–Lagos flight. After the doors had been shut, he then maintained a two-way communication with the simulator crew externally. About fifty-five minutes later, the supposed flight touched down in Lagos and taxied to the parking ramp. At this point, the gentleman went into the rhetoric of how thankful he was to the pilots, with the usual liturgy of flattery. Finally, he rounded off with a sermon on how things would have been so disastrous for him if not for them. In the closing remarks from the crew, they thanked him very much for the plenitude of his compliments and bade him farewell too.

As soon as the door was opened and he disembarked at the fictitious Lagos ramp, everywhere was dark, but he was still able to wave to a few faces he recognised, totally oblivious of his real environment until his instructor friend appeared and welcomed him to Lagos. It was gathered that the administrative officer did not show any surprise about his instructor friend's presence in Lagos. He even thought that the simulator facility corridor he was actually walking through was the Muritala Mohammed Airport local arrival wing until he got to the end of the corridor only to find the taxi park immediately in front of the arrival hall missing. It was then that he turned around to ask his simulator instructor friend what was going on. The instructor smiled triumphantly and unfolded the whole so-called mystery to him. I might as well add here that during our jet transition training with United Airlines there was a joke that reflected the marvel of flight simulation. An American pilot said the simulator had made pilots the only group of mortals that broke Jesus Christ's record of resurrection in the sense that certain manoeuvres in the simulator sometimes led to a "crash". The pilot then "died" after the simulated crash only to resurrect as soon as the simulator instructor had reset the equipment. Usually the resetting of equipment took a period of ten to twenty minutes at most.

Meanwhile, our Lord Jesus Christ spent seventy-two hours in achieving this feat.

Another incident that corroborates the consummate realism of flight simulation occurred during the simulator phase of an A310 training programme. Members of a Nigeria Airways crew were undergoing their final simulator check, and the captain was doing the flying. During the check, for some inexplicable reason, the captain "crashed" the airplane thrice within thirty minutes of the scheduled two-hour check. The now very worried French instructor told the captain that since the company owned four of the airplanes and the captain had crashed three of them so far, then logically if he crashed one more he would have crashed all the A310 owned, and of course that sure would signify the end of the training for the crew. Thank God the captain didn't crash the fourth airplane.

After the overflowing wellspring of misinformation about what to expect of the simulator phase of the training programme, we finally left Lagos for Denver, Colorado, where the United Airlines training facility was located. Our departure was on WT 850 non-stop service to New York in August 1981. The flight was quite a pleasant trip that took about ten hours and thirty minutes. The cabin entertainment was very nice. Apart from this, for one reason or another, any pilot course in Nigeria Airways attracted so much attention within the community that one would not be too wrong to say that it was news per se. I was not familiar with the cabin staff on that trip, but to my surprise they knew us and also what our mission was all about and politely wished us the best. This was unsettling and soothing at the same time. We spent a night in New York Milford Plaza Hotel in the so-called Big Apple area of the city. The following day we caught the Eastern Airline Service to Denver, Colorado. During the airplane's final descent into Colorado Airport, the jet tales rushed back to my mind. The only aspect that I actually gave serious thought to was the speed of the jet airplane compared to the much slower F27 turboprop airplane. I had come to realise during the type-rating training on the F27 that a great transition in speed often made the task of accomplishing the objectives of a type endorsement quite difficult. I recall vividly that while in flight training school, after the twin-engine Cessna 310 which had a maximum cruising speed of 160 kts, it was sweat all the way trying to cope with the F27 cruising speed of about 250 kts, especially with the F27 being a higher performing airplane than the Cessna 310. The trouble is always at the initial stage of the training where things happen so fast that one usually ends up falling behind the airplane's pace, which means that the airplane is flying you rather than you flying the airplane. Sometimes during training one feels so bad that one starts entertaining grave doubts about one's status as a pilot.

In summary, the speed difference transition between the Cessna and the F27 then was a paltry 90 kts, but this time around (i.e. F27/B737) we were talking about a speed transition of over 110 kts. Secondly, there was a difference in performance, and also a weight difference of over 10,000 kg amongst other things. These were the only aspects that occupied my thoughts. As for flight simulation, I had had experience of that during my training as flight engineer on the B727 turbo jet which I got certified on. So, my main worry was how soon it would take to overcome the speed thing in accordance with the scheduled training period. My total experience so far was 478 flying hours of which 209 was logged on the F27 airplane. Basically, this put me in the category of a low-time pilot, so to speak. It was in full cognisance of this that I prepared quite well beforehand to master, at least, the technical information about the B737 airplane. The airplane, in general, is a twin-jet transport airplane designed for short- and medium-range operation. It is 100 ft long and has a 93 ft wing span. The maximum operating airspeed of the plane is 350 kts or 0.84 Mach. The term Mach, simply put, is the ratio of an airplane's true airspeed to the local speed of sound. The speed of sound itself is generally assumed as 600 kts or Mach 1. Lastly, the B737 airplane has a maximum certificated altitude of 35,000 ft.

Deplaning at Colorado International Airport, we walked across to the baggage hall and waited around the carrousel for our luggage. The airport was just another international airport in the western world. The only scene I still recollect was the large gathering of Americans wearing such different shapes and sizes of cowboy hats. It was an interesting scene that wound my mind back to those Western cowboy movies I had watched. It also made me ask myself whether The Duke or Mr John Wayne, was born there. In brief, it was my first cultural education about the people of Denver, Colorado. As soon as we got out of the airport's terminal building, we had a hotel bus waiting to convey us to the hotel. The trip to the hotel was a pleasant one. The scenery en route was quite impressive. Well, it was the usual American suburban set-up, i.e. beautiful lawns, serene environment and impressive architectural designs. As soon as we got to the hotel we found out much to our surprise that we had been allocated rooms already. All we did was to sign for the room keys we picked up from the front desk. So far, efficiency was at work. Waiting for us in the rooms were papers delineating our course schedule and programme. Things were really happening fast.

The following morning, the hotel bus conveyed us to the United Airline Training Institute. The premises had a high and reinforced entrance gate with an armed security official taking care of all entry protocol. The security official had radio contact with all the different departmental offices housed in the premises. After a few minutes' dialogue on his communication box with some office in the premises he handed each of us a security pass valid for the duration of our training programme. He then opened the electrically-controlled gate and directed us to a building that turned out to be the operations department. At the operations office we introduced ourselves to a lady seated at a desk with her name and the inscription "Secretary to the Operations Manager" displayed on the plaque in front of her. She soon announced our arrival to her boss (who had been expecting us) and showed us into his office. Inside the office was seated a gentleman, probably in his late forties or early fifties, with some well trimmed grey hair, and wearing a beautifully tailored suit. As soon as we entered, he stood up, shook hands with us and inquired about our flying experience so far. All the while he was quite business-like, until he figured out that we were just a bunch of low-time pilots on jet transition training, when he began to admonish us on the need to work towards successful completion of our training programme.

I recall his saying something like, "Gentlemen, with your level of experience, I shouldn't mince words in telling you that the

B737 training curriculum by United Airlines standards requires a lot of hard work and total concentration throughout the entire course programme. With these also, your public relations and personal conduct with your different instructors, and your relationship with the entire staff within these premises, form part of your final grading and type endorsement. Gentlemen, in airline career flying, the employer places a lot of emphasis on individual attitudes. I must tell you that even if you turn out to be some virtuoso pilot, with a bad attitude no passenger airline would ever give your so-called skill precocity any thought, because it's through your personality and self-conduct that the company to an extent gets advertised."

He also observed that the most difficult period for the airline pilot is while he is still working towards logging 1,500 hours of flying experience. He had arrived at this conclusion in his over two decades in the operations department. He said so many other helpful things before we went into the official protocol of documentation and collection of all the manuals we needed for the entire programme. This chap is one fellow I will never forget, as far as career flying goes.

I remember his allowing us free access to his office at any time we encountered difficulty during the programme. Then he gave us a tip about what to expect during the simulator phase of the programme. He told us that no matter how fine the progress during the simulator sessions, it had been gathered from research that there would be this particular session when the trainee would just do everything wrong to the extent that he would almost want to give up. He advised us to remember this and be on the watch out for it. The phenomenon was commonplace during transition training. He told us in a matter-of-fact tone that there was no escaping this, as long as one was flying the jet for the first time. He even got metaphorical and compared it to the no-escape pain syndrome of "disvirginising" a woman. That made the whole message sink in quite well.

After the counselling, the documentation and the eventual tour of the training premises, we went back to the hotel, changed, and hit the streets of Denver. It was TGIF (thank God it's Friday), and we were supposed to be back in school for Monday. I had missed America since I left school in California in 1979, so it was red paint all the way, and I was ready to paint like hell. To tell you how qualified I was as a painter then, I was twenty-three years old, very single, free and virile, and I had as pecuniary capital from Nigeria Airways a total sum of over $6,000. The rest can be imagined. Regretfully, the two days of bliss went by quite fast. By Monday, the thought of now going to face the real business stultified the whole euphoria of having been back in the USA, and in summertime too. As a matter of fact, the short trip to school in the hotel bus made the whole feeling very evanescent. The nearer we got to the training premises, the more the small talk among us diminished, until the whole cabin was finally silent. As boxer Larry Homes used to say, "Sparring is different from the real thing." We had done all our sparring telling tales, now here came the real thing. It was either a case of jet castration or jet "uhuru". Suddenly, I became a staunch Christian. I prayed hard for God's guidance and an overall success. The silence in the bus cabin became almost audible. It did not require a course in mind reading to figure out that the terse silence was brought on by the impact of the real business that we were going to face just a couple of minutes away now.

Well, the first day in school wasn't that bad. We were to undergo a one-week mandatory UAL integration course for all pilots. The course was quite academic in content and we could be classified as adult education students; pilot training or not, our course was just another TWI (training within industry) as far as the company as a whole was concerned. Of course, most TWIs are usually adult training. By the civil aviation laws, since the B737 airplane is a two-man crew cockpit in composition and complement, for all the programme phases all that needed to be done had to be done by the crew in pairs. Already I had my own partner with whom I had enjoyed a cordial relationship while flying the F27. He was a God-sent partner, in the sense that we had built a very good relationship which became the subject of discussions among our set composition. During the F27 days, I had come to revere my friend's flying dexterity, which to date remains unequalled by anybody else. His only handicap was an aversion to technical details or any academic information.

Conversely, he knew my technical ability and had come to respect that. So we were a perfect pair, more or less. In academics, I was his able back-up, and when we got to the flight simulation stage, he was my able back-up. The one-week integration course was a refresher type course, reminiscent of the Zaria syllabus. The course was a revisitation of the ground school subjects studied while in the flight training school. But the mode of instruction was a completely new dimension in flight training. The class was more or less a computer room. All the students' desks in the room had installed on them a full cathode ray tube (CRT) screen and a teleprinter computer set. As a matter of fact, the room was generally referred to as PLATO (Personnel and Pilots' Computer Training Facility) room. The only physical presence of people apart from the student were in PLATO facility hands that played the role of aides. The course subjects were devoluted through the computer interface or the CRT screen, where, after storing your password in the computer database, execution of the password and recalling it gave you access to the stored course programme menu. It was my first time being instructed through a computer medium, and it was a very welcome training concept. The password which was personal and private to the student provided access to the menu and closure of the subject matter studied at the end of the day. Your password was like a savings account number (that is to say, only you could withdraw from it and also close the account). The subject matter was devoluted visually through the interface screen of the computer's CRT, while the audio channel could be heard from a headset installed on the student's desk. The beauty of the training was in its duration of one week. The course had nine subjects, in each of which an 80% score would activate the artificial grading intelligence of the PLATO to reflect your mastery of the subject on the screen. Thereafter, the information was stored in its central database located somewhere in the state of Texas, USA. I remember completing my programme one day ahead of schedule. One other rare occurrence at the facility was the presence of an Apollo module astronaut. Having spent two days in the facility, our group and the PLATO hands had got so friendly that we now enjoyed a wider freedom of movement around the premises, and indulged in conversation (though this was not allowed). But the day of the astronaut's presence was a different one. I noticed that the PLATO hands kept insisting that we keep our voices down, and we naturally wanted to know why. So, one of the hands mentioned the presence of the astronaut to us, pointing towards him, and we just stared at the dual-planet being with fascination and awe. We asked the PLATO hand if we could get the astronaut's autograph, but to our dismay she told us the astronaut was there on an important assignment to make corrections and update some information stored in the PLATO database. I recall the PLATO hand telling us that during one of his previous visits to PLATO, the astronaut had flunked a question in aerodynamics. She said with a chuckle that it had been a big surprise to everybody present. In this brief encounter, I learnt the need to be as conservative as possible in one's esteem of global personalities, often shaped by the glorified pictures of slick personalities painted by journalists in newspapers and magazines. The astronaut looked regular enough, so regular that we only recognised his presence after his identity had been revealed. But of course, the human mind being what it is, the man still appeared ethereal to me, and the absolute silence he maintained throughout his stay was moon-like in nature.

Well, on completion of the one-week PLATO course, we moved on to attend the three-week B737 systems ground school course. The PLATO concept adopted by UAL in the pilots' integration training programme was a big marvel to me. The concept was quite efficacious. Career-wise, the PLATO experience came to be the solid base in my storage and information source that earned me most of my career achievements. The PLATO syndrome hit me so hard that I came to accept computer technology as the only flawless medium of instruction in the sense that the human factor, which often compromised results, had been totally eradicated. It was with this blissful thought that I looked forward to a more advanced mode of instruction in the airplane system's ground school course. In all sincerity, with the PLATO experience, I had long concluded that encountering a human being as an instructor would come at the flight simulation phase of the airplane programme. I was looking forward to a programmed *robot* as the teaching medium and guide for the system ground school. Unfortunately, this was not to be. The ground school instructor was a man. That made the whole class climate the business-as-usual type.

The solace though was that the teaching aids installed in the classroom reduced the frequency of dialogue with the instructor to the barest minimum. Apart from the instructor, other teaching aids used included the blackboard and the slide screen with the film cassette connected to it. The slide's audio could be heard from headsets on each student's desk if properly tuned to the slide's audio frequency. At the end of every topic, multiple-choice questions were reflected on the slide screen. Through the audio channel, a recorded voice read out the question reflected on the slide screen and then gave a three-minute pause for each student to answer the question by thumbing buttons marked according to the alphabetical arrangement of the multiple answers on the slide screen. Whether the student was correct or not, the audio would read the correct answer as shown in the next slide picture that came after the three-minute pause. Whatever choice of answer each student made was reflected on a general console on the instructor's table. The instructor (before the answer slide changed) then went ahead to explain why the slide's choice of answer was the right one.

The first day in the airplane system class turned eventful only about fifteen minutes into the scheduled six-hour period of lecture time per day. After the ground school instructor had written his name on the blackboard and introduced himself, he welcomed us in transparent politeness. His attitude towards us was soon confirmed by the first picture that came on the slide screen. The picture depicted the cockpit of the B737 airplane with two headset wearing monkeys seated in the two crew seats. He made the picture stay for a few seconds before he switched on to the next slide picture which now depicted the airplane itself. The audio announced the commencement of the system training course. As for that first slide picture, I just didn't know the interpretation I was supposed to give to it. Many opprobrious thoughts were racing through my mind. What actually set my adrenaline flowing was the derisive way the monkeys were staring at us and smiling too. My grouse was: why a cockpit crew of monkeys? Especially in a class of humans and skilled professionals. The risk in flying any airplane is too clear for anybody to look at it as some monkey business. I just couldn't catch the drift of that picture. But it sure spoilt my own day. The fact that the instructor himself feigned ignorance of that picture and offered no explanation for it made the whole thing disappointingly dirty. If that was supposed to be some form of humour, then in my honest opinion, predicated on my knowledge (acquired through the textbook and the physical experience of having lived and schooled in the USA) of the vast racial problem in America, especially between whites and blacks, this humourless humour was surely an oxymoron, to say the least. In the ocean of global politics, racism occupies a very volatile and highly flammable category. The picture did one thing to me though. It made me resolved that the onus was now on me to prove the picture otherwise by making sure I succeeded, thereby turning the picture to just another natural joke of the heroic failure type.

Later on, though, the class turned out to be an interesting experience as the systems instruction went on. There were, all together, nine system topics, and I must say that due to the first time encounter with some technical terms, some of my colleagues showed so much ignorance that it was impossible to hold back from laughing sometimes. The first incident of this nature came when we were treating the electrical system of the airplane. I for one was expecting this situation, because it had happened to me during the programme for my certification as flight engineer on the B727 turbojet. So it was now my turn to sit back and enjoy the innocent but funny enquiries about some technical terms. Most turbojets do the storage, change, and transfer of electrical power, through electrical bus units. The literature on these units contains information on the airplane's electrical systems. So, if the story was not about the battery bus, it was about the bus tie-breaker, then transfer bus, then DC bus, then standby bus, and so many other buses, which finally made a colleague of mine get so bussed (he probably had municipal buses running up and down in his mind) after the second day of the bus route web, so to speak, that he opened up to me and confessed that the bus thing wasn't making any sense to him, but was only giving him nightmares. I had to now simplify the bus concept to him, before he was able to get on with the course. This pleasure-pain fun continued throughout the rest of the course. After three weeks, we went on to the next phase of the programme, which, this time, was the cockpit procedure trainer (CPT) phase.

The Cockpit Trainer

This training equipment is, in design and concept, reminiscent of the aims and objective of the flight simulator. The CPT programme was for one week. The equipment is some kind of crude simulator, or put differently a dummy-type simulator. The training in this equipment prepares a pilot for the more cumbersome task frequently encountered in the simulator. The CPT equipment is built in a way similar to the airplane cockpit, with all the cockpit's instruments installed. The missing link is the non-provision of digital computer technology, so that the manipulation of controls is done manually. This is to improve the pilot's cockpit set-up and scan flow and also enable him to ask questions regarding the airplane system. After the instructor has assessed a pilot as attaining the speed in all the manoeuvres to be practised in the real flight simulator, he then gets signed off to continue to the almighty flight simulator. I completed my CPT training with my partner in three days. This created a four-day period of respite for us before starting the simulator programme.

The B737 Simulator Experience

The B737 simulator training is a ten-lesson training session of practice in normal and emergency/abnormal and non-normal procedural actions, at each crew member's assigned cockpit task. The objective of the course is to emphasise flight safety, passenger comfort and operational efficiency.

Four days after successful completion of the CPT phase, my partner and I were scheduled to commence our flight simulator session at 1.00 a.m. local time in Denver. Usually, flight crews spend a total of four hours per simulator session or lesson, with a bifurcation of 50% of the total period spent between the pair of crew. Also, before entering the simulator facility, the simulator instructor and his students would have spent an hour reviewing the lesson for the session, strictly following the reflected format on the lesson paper. Now, remember, my partner and I already had a nexus of contract in role trade. So far I had delivered my own part, and very well too. This was now his own part and coincidentally, the final execution of the contract. As far as airplane flying is concerned, he was my hero. So I looked up to him at this phase of the programme the way a child looks up to his father. The morning of our first simulator session went quite fine. The lesson format was straightforward and simple enough. The context was basically an assessment of the students' instrument flying capability of the B737 airplane. On arrival at the facility premises that morning, we had waiting for us our instructor, who introduced himself, and as we announced our names in turn he checked these off on the list he had been furnished with. Satisfied, he led us into the B737 briefing room and got down to business. As the instructor had a problem pronouncing our names, we agreed he could address us by our first names. He then requested us to tell him about our flying experience so far and what type of airplane we had each flown last. As he gathered that this was going to be our first jet experience, he became quite meticulous and explicit in explaining the lesson for the day. He probed the level of technical knowledge we had obtained of the airplane, and after an hour of further instructions he finally led us into the simulator facility. Quite incidentally, my partner was chosen to do the first flying. I think this might have been because of his obvious excitement and eagerness to get started, betrayed by his utterances during the pre-simulator briefing. He walked so briskly towards the simulator chosen for our use among numerous others inside the big simulator premises that he even got to the box before the instructor and me. As for me, all that was perfectly in order as far as my partner was concerned. He had been itching for this moment since the day we arrived in Denver. I recalled him even wandering into the simulator premises during the CPT, feigning loss of direction.

As for me, I was sure the instructor easily noticed my lack of enthusiasm as I walked towards the simulator. He probably also noticed that the situation got worse as we got closer to the facility.

My partner was going to fly first, so he had to occupy the right seat, since we were being trained for the first officer position on the airplane. In that case, he would now be the pilot flying (PF), while I would have to sit on the left seat, to carry out the duties of pilot not flying (PNF). The first lesson was basic instrument flying, with demonstration of the airplane characteristics under certain conditions, i.e. her acceleration and deceleration rates, which might sometimes lead to undesirable situations if for some reason the crew exceeded or fell short of the maximum and minimum speed limits of the airplane. We practised the recovery procedure for these situations. My partner, as I expected, put up such a good performance that the instructor asked him once again if he was actually flying the jet airplane for the first time. He did so well that during his two-hour period that he never had to repeat any of the itemised manoeuvres on the lesson format. I was very proud of him.

After he had completed his own scheduled two hours, we left the simulator box and took a five-minute break, during which we fooled around with the facility's vending machine, which stocked a variety of snacks with hot and cold drinks as one chose. Five minutes later, we were back in the simulator box, and this time around I was the PF and I occupied the right seat. The moment I did my first take-off the jet comedy started. For the first twenty minutes of the two-hour period I just couldn't get any single parameter under control. Funnily enough, and unusually for me, I didn't feel anything about the fumbling. I knew it was my subconscious mind that was at play. All day long I had fed into my subconscious that possibility of failing to perform well at the simulator and this was now manifesting physically. Well, I had to repeat some manoeuvres, and in the end my performance in comparison with my partner's was far from being on a par. As in the 7-Up jingle, the difference was clear! I must say, though, that it was the crystallisation of the earlier jet tales, coupled with the unexpected and overwhelming circus of switches and lights reminiscent of the Christmas tree and lighting culture, that actually blew me into a twenty-minute episode of the *jet scare*. Also, since the programme started, it had been a synthesis of information from manuals, component sketches and diagrams, in concert later on with the dummy switches of the CPT. All these had led to imaginative streams of thought which finally came together in the simulator box.

Before I go on, I must say that I would always remember that my partner's elation was reflected in his total sublimation from his morbid indignation at all the academic details we had gone through since the programme started to his rare and personally blissful euphoria of the simulator. The simulator environment, I soon found out, was just his natural habitat. His precocity in the handling of airplanes was fully exhibited here. His earlier performance on the day of the first lesson had a dual effect on the instructor in the sense that he affected that our performance as a pair was average, and also he came to appreciate the training standard of our company in view of our low-time category as pilots, though it was as clear as glass who had the hegemony.

Let me digress a bit. During the period my partner and I served on the F27 as co-pilots, I must say that the major disparity we had skill-wise was the inherent airplane handling and fast learning ability that he possessed. Even with this, in the long run I always ended up abeam him skill-wise, but his being able to apply a better polish to his skill made him shine better. As far as attaining the required and lawful standard went, we were very much at par.

Well, we soon entered the second day, and this time around, I sat as the PF for the first of the two-hour sessions of the day. The instructor made sure I repeated some instructed manoeuvres in which he felt I had not attained the required standard to make me progress into lesson two of the course. By the time I finally attained this and moved on to lesson two manoeuvres, I realised sadly that I was just thirty-three minutes away from the end of my scheduled two hours. Consequently, I was only able to accomplish (successfully though) just 25% of the itemised manoeuvres for lesson two before we went for the coffee break. Naturally, I was now behind on the course. The feeling of that alone almost tempted me to ask the instructor if I could trade my coffee break to enable me to get on with the lesson. It was only wishful thinking, for in aviation I had come to learn that rules were rules. Once rules are followed, things usually unfold for the better.

The five-minute break was a big drag for me throughout the full flight simulation programme. The reason was simply an unfortunate case of fate once more. This was because most of our session schedules were in the early hours of the day. During this period of the day, the vending machine only served coffee, which occupied a permanent number in my "no drinks" list. So the break time was to me clearly not a coffee break, but a five-minute interlude to silently and rapidly rehearse all the manoeuvres on the lesson format if I was going to be the PF after the break, or, conversely, to assess my last performance if I had been PF first, and either scold myself or at least smile over any progress made.

So my partner was now the PF, and as expected he was doing quite fine until about an hour and ten minutes into the second lesson when things suddenly fell apart. What happened hit us both like a sledgehammer. When the whole episode was considered in retrospect, it had to be acknowledged that this was a trainee who hadn't flown a jet airplane before but whose progress so far had been phenomenal.

The instructor (as he later admitted to us just a day before the end of the entire simulator programme) decided, using his wealth of experience in simulator instruction, to make my partner's progress and rise in confidence meteoric. In doing this, he had to simulate some manoeuvres that would be completely beyond the control of my partner and make him eventually experience the worst nightmare for any pilot, which is crashing an airplane. Incidentally, when you do crash in the simulator, the events and the final simulation of the crash are so real in the simulator box that sometimes one might have to be held down or reminded by the simulator instructor that one was in a simulator box and not in the real airplane. Sometimes after a crash in the simulator, one just felt like going home to look forward to the next and hopefully a better day.

So that was it. My partner was flying very well and the instructor failed the left engine. As PNF, I called out the failure to the PF, but before I could finish with the callout, bang!, we were in a 60 degree bank with the speed dropping like hell. A few seconds later, there were unbearable vibrations that evolved finally into that unmistakable noise of the airplane structure blasting or exploding into fragments. It was our first experience of a simulator crash and it sure felt real. At the moment of this *nouveau* and stampede experience, my able partner who was now in a state of total quandary, gave me a death-like glance and stultified the already uncomfortable and eerie feeling I had of being drowned, by bursting into a long soliloquy in his native Hausa Fulani dialect. This got the instructor and me not only confused but scared. The instructor was totally at a loss. Knowing my partner quite well, I was expecting him to do something irrational to the instructor. That was what he did sometimes during line flights with some captains when we were still flying the F27 if something rather embarrassing like this happened to him. As long as he felt he was not the cause, he immediately followed up with a commensurate measure of reprisal. So, as for his next move, my worry was for the instructor. The moment he recovered from his "audible trance", so to speak, the first thing he did was to ask me what actually happened. I simply told him: "We just crashed, friend, we lost number one engine." Thank God, he just shook his head in amazement, looked at the instructor and requested for an immediate repetition of that manoeuvre. Unfortunately though, by the time the simulator could be reset with other actions required to reproduce the manoeuvre, the schedule was already up.

Leaving the simulator box, the instructor explained to us in detail what had happened. He also helped to lift our now alarmingly low morale when he said that for the phase of flight during which he introduced the manoeuvre, he expected just what happened in view of our being alien to the yaw characteristics of the B737 airplane, which could be an unforgiving airplane under this condition if the crew experiencing the condition are not well trained for the recovery procedure.

Well, while the instructor was busy debriefing us, I was thinking that if my hero could go down like this with this alien manoeuvre, I might as well not show up for the third lesson because the format was full of this particular manoeuvre. Also, I was about forty minutes behind already, so I sure wouldn't like to make a further mockery of myself by adding two hours more to my backward stance. But I felt I should show up all the same, even if only to have the instructor and my partner go through the trauma of watching me star in the bad movie that I knew the lesson was going to be for me. On the way to our hotel, my friend probably still befuddled about the simulator incident, said, "Hey, Ty, that bloke sure caught me hands down." I knew he was going to say something like this because his principle, as far as handling an airplane went, was that whenever he erred, no matter how small the fault was, he would quickly try to get off the fault in the shortest time possible. I said to him: "My friend, you are complaining of being caught hands down. Just wait till tomorrow, when I will not only be caught both hands and pants down but will also be formally interned." Then, without realising what I was doing, I started muttering to myself in pidgin English as I was looking out of the bus window that I had been advised to go to medical school by my parents but stupidly I had demurred only to put myself in this calamity at this late hour in my life.

When my friend told me about this later, he said what had bothered him with all my verbal insanity was that as soon as I stopped muttering, I never uttered another word. We shared the same hotel room, and although he tried so hard to get me to speak while in the room, I just whispered the word "jet" quietly under my breath and jumped into bed without even changing my clothes. To his utmost surprise, it was a matter of minutes before I started snoring. When he recounted this incident over breakfast the following morning and was making fun of me, I just shocked him too by mentioning his tutoring the instructor and me in his mother tongue in the simulator for some minutes after he had given the airplane the worst fuselage slam. Then he said, "Oh yeah? Is that right?"

I said, "Don't 'oh yeah?' me!" I told him that he was smart enough to have gone to his roots verbally and that he should stop harassing me. Then I said to him: "Look, friend, do we really have to fly a jet airplane? We were doing quite fine on the props. Pity they got sold. As for me now, I have resolved to jet out the idea of flying the jet." He got very serious, looked at me and said one abusive word in my native dialect that eventually made me hold my peace. In the spirit of our eternal friendship he mentioned some names of fellow professional colleagues who were in the

UNITED

CAPTAIN (CIRCLE ONE)					
(F/O) S/O T.O. FATUNGASE		DOMICILE NIGERIA	FILE NUMBER	☑ AIRPLANE	☒ P/C
				☑ VISUAL SIM	☐ P/T
AIRCRAFT TYPE & NUMBER B-737/9265	BLOCK TIME :25	FLIGHT TIME :21	SIMULATOR TIME 1:30	☐ SIMULATOR	☐ RECHECK
				☑ ORAL	☐ RATING
OBSERVER		GRADING LEGEND		☐ (200 · 1/2)	☐ SPECIAL
ORAL		S - Satisfactory		☐ (CAT II)	☐ EVAC.
S/M		U - Unsatisfactory		☐ PREFLIGHT	☐ DITCHING (INITIAL) (RECURR)
A/C		I - Incomplete (Other than proficiency)			
NUMBER PC LANDINGS ACCOMPLISHED IN APPROVED SIMULATOR					

REMARKS

SIMULATOR CHECK MANEUVERS — ENGINE FAIL ON TAKEOFF, ILS,
NON PRECISION APPROACH, STALLS, REJECTED TAKE OFF, AREA
DEPARTURE, AREA ARRIVAL, HOLDING

ROBERT G. STAGGS   ATP # 1371193
U.A.L F/I

This flight crew member has been checked/trained as indicated above. Applicable provisions of all Federal Air Regulations and the UAL Flight Training Manual have been met when satisfactorily completed.

BRIEF TIME	TRAINING TIME	ADF	ILS	BK CRS	VOR	RADAR APP	CHECK FLIGHT ENGINEER SIGNATURE	DATE
1:30	4:55 TOTAL 21:36 P/C	S	S	S	S	S		
PART 121 APPROVED INSTRUCTOR R C Staggs						DATE 8/29/81	EVACUATION TRAINING INSTRUCTOR SIGNATURE	DATE
CHECK AIRMAN (S/M) SIGNATURE R C Staggs						DATE 8/29/81	DITCHING INSTRUCTOR SIGNATURE	DATE
CHECK AIRMAN (A/C) SIGNATURE						DATE 9/11/81	FLIGHT OFFICER SIGNATURE fatungase	
CHECK AIRMAN (ORAL) SIGNATURE R C Staggs						DATE 8/29/81	REVIEWED BY MANAGER/DIRECTOR OF FLIGHT OPERATIONS	
UO 108 REV 9-79 PRINTED IN U.S.A.								

SIMULATOR PROFICIENCY CHECK FORMAT

SIMULATOR SKETCH

company and operating in the substantive position of First Officers, on this same B737 jet airplane.

He enthused in a matter-of-fact tone: "Ty, by Allah, if these guys could make this training, then we should do even better."

I responded "Amen" after he had said "Insha Allah." Case closed. I was going to the end.

Now before I go on with the details of the progress of our de facto programme, I would like to treat in detail a normal simulator lesson format, taking the inventory of the format items one by one. I must point out here that though these lesson formats are designed to suit the training concept of the particular airline, whatever training concept an airline adopts must be approved by the Civil Aviation Authority (CAA) in concert with airplane manufacturers. This ensures that standards required by law are common to all operators. This is the regulation. The emphasis on safety in the aviation business involves the CAA, airplane manufacturers, airplane operators (that is, the airliners) and pilots, among others. The manufacturer prescribes the procedure to be used by all trained flight crews. If for any reason during flight operations a situation arises where the captain feels a deviation from prescribed procedure is imminent, he must deviate in such a way that logic and good judgement remain the bottom line of his action. For the purpose of clearly explaining what the simulator lesson is all about, I shall naturally be using the UAL simulator lesson format as a reference.

The Simulator Lesson

In explaining the nature of a typical simulator session, I find it necessary to use the simulator lesson usually prepared for the final simulator check. The final simulator check is a cumulative grill of all manoeuvres that have been practised from the onset of the simulator programme.

The training sketch contains vast information regarding the day-to-day grading of both the simulator lesson and the real airplane training. I did my simulator check on the 28th of August, 1981. Most of the manoeuvres are similar to those discussed in the section of this book that examines a pilot's typical day. To make the present discussion easier, I shall only touch the unfamiliar aspects. The procedure is basically the same as the procedure for manoeuvres on the F27 airplane. The only visible difference is in speed. On a jet airplane, things happen at a faster pace. We will examine unfamiliar manoeuvres like (1) engine failure before V2; (2) APU fire; and (3) Asymmetrical Training Edge Devices (TED). Before proceeding, let me mention here that in both airplane simulator and real flight training, the checklist booklet (once again) and the airplane flight operations manual play a very vital role in the process of carrying out a particular manoeuvre in the prescribed manner.

Engine Failure Before V2

Twin-engine airplanes of whatever category, class or type are all prone to the "yaw phenomenon" once the airplane engines start producing asymmetrical thrust. This subsequently leads to a "yawing moment" commensurate with the uneven thrust output of the engines. The "yawing characteristic" of an airplane (that is, whether it is the moderate or violent type) depends on the location of the power plant on the airplane's structure and the amount of thrust being generated by the engines. It is logical to expect that if an airplane's thrust output is great, then the yawing moment during any asymmetrical thrust condition should equally be great. This sounds quite in order, but truly speaking, this is not so. Also, twin-engine airplanes with engines attached to their wing structure produce more yawing moment compared to airplanes with their twin engines located at the tail area of the airplane. So the condition that can cause the worst yawing moments for a twin-engine airplane is the total loss of thrust in either engine (which is usually an engine failure). In our case, since the jet engine produced a relatively high thrust propulsion, the chances were that in the situation of an engine loss, the yaw we are talking about is analogous in character to that effect which causes a motor car in motion to veer sideways suddenly when she suffers a sudden improper tyre alignment, for example in a blow-out. This is so because, due to the difference in pressure from the tyres, the car tends to drag to one side during motion (since the tyre pressure difference is now asymmetrical).

Now, the B737-200 is a twin-engine jet airplane fitted with Pratt and Whitney engines located beneath the wing structure of the airplane and producing 15,000 lbs of thrust each. The engine on the port side is number one, while the one on the starboard is number two. The engines have been given this identification for clarity, and because of some engineering and maintenance factors. This numbering system is a general norm in virtually all of the free western world.

So talking about our subject matter (i.e. engine failure at V2), this manoeuvre was adopted as part of the pilot's training because the transient phase of airplane rotation and subsequent acceleration to the V2 (or safety) speed is generally considered one of the most critical phases of flight. This is logically so in the sense that at this take-off phase of flight execution, the airplane has just lifted off the runway and the landing gear (i.e. that assembly module of iron rods with tyre fittings at the base which makes the ground motion of the airplane possible during the ground manoeuvre referred to as taxiing) is probably in transit towards full retraction and the take-off flaps are still deployed. These components now quickly start inducing drag, as whatever was formerly lift-enhancing reverts to a drag-inducing surface once lift-off is accomplished. Thus, if an engine is to fail at this stage, the chances are that the airplane will go bang!

For the B737 airplane, when this occurs, the PF doesn't need to be told because, right there and then, quite a few things would start going haywire both in the plane's motion and on the PF instrument panel, plus the fact that the pilot's failure to react promptly would inevitably lead to a disaster. Well, this situation is considered by the airplane manufacturers to be quite abnormal for any trained and certified flight crew. This, of course, is absolutely true. For the PF, the first indication of an engine failure while airborne is roll detection of an engine, and the PF instinctively makes a heading change. Simultaneously, the PNF (by procedure) is duty-bound to call out this abnormality as soon as it is recognised. This is a reflection of the globally adopted crew concept that pilots are able back-ups for each other in all phases of flight execution. Thank

God this concept starts and ends during flight execution, because if this had been extended to the crew's social life, too, I know some perverted colleagues who would exploit this concept by making love to another colleague's wife, all in the name of that concept. And if the context of the concept's application was unlimited, that colleague would be enjoying full legal protection. I am sure also that this concept alone would have had most airlines deluged with monomaniacs with very vicious libido problems hiding under the umbrella of being pilots to realise morbid ambitions, exploiting the law of course.

Once a pilot detects a heading change not induced by him during a manual flight, he knows immediately by virtue of his training that his airplane is under a yaw condition. His first reaction, by recall and procedure wise, is to get the airplane back on her original flight path. In our situation, the PF can only gain control of the airplane's flight path by countering the yaw condition with the smooth application of the airplane's rudder pedals and simultaneously maintaining a safe speed (V2) so that he may achieve a rather shallow climb to an altitude where he can now put the airplane in a level flight so that he may be able, and safely too, to retract the take-off flaps on schedule and accelerate to a safe manoeuvring speed. As per the recommended procedure for this manoeuvre, all recovery actions must be done according to the laid down sequence. In following this sequence by recall, the PF on recognition of this problem would call out for the landing gear retraction (usually clashing with the PNF call-out of positive rate of climb) while simultaneously applying the rudder pedal to counteract the yaw. As soon as he climbs the aircraft to 800 ft above the field elevation, he now levels out the airplane at this height and, thereafter, he starts retracting the take-off flaps on schedule while the airplane is gradually accelerating. After the final take-off flap retraction, the PF waits for the airplane to attain the flaps up manoeuvring speed for the airplane (in this case, 210 kts indicated airspeed) and then commands the PNF to set the maximum continuous thrust value on the live engine and thereafter he calls out for the engine-failure-and-shut-down checklist to be read. The PNF now responds by reading out aloud all the items on that checklist to verify that the necessary actions have been accomplished. As soon as he calls the checklist complete, the PF requests the after-take-off checklist and simultaneously informs the PNF about his intention to try and restart the engine by calling for the in-flight-engine-start checklist. If after this the engine still cannot be regained, the next action is for a re-clearance request to come back for a landing from the ATC. Usually, express clearance is given to airplanes under any abnormal condition. The clearance in this type of situation contains mainly the present active runway and the type of let-down approach in use. With the clearance fully copied and understood, the PF, while complying with the clearance, requests the descent-approach checklist with one engine inoperative. Most checklist items under the abnormal checklist are the read-and-do type. That is why in any situation under the abnormal category, the flight crew must try as much as possible not to be in too much of a hurry. Trying to hurry things up usually leads to hurrying to forget or carry out an action properly. With all actions completed for that abnormal condition, the first manoeuvre as far as this particular condition is concerned is to align the airplane on the final approach course for the active runway, and, the moment the PF feels certain about making the runway, he orders the landing gear extension (having selected both the primary and intermediate flaps during the descent approach phase of the manoeuvre) and simultaneously the final landing flap setting for the particular configuration. He then calls for the one-engine-inoperative-landing checklist. The checklist would be read by the PNF who must make sure that the PF responds rightly and of course does the right thing too. The PNF then calls the checklist complete and the rest now for them is landing as soon as they get clearance to land from the ATC. The PNF now makes standard call out, generally centred upon any slight deviation from the established flight path. As soon as the landing is made, the PF now goes into the braking action and procedure for stopping the airplane. That ends the trauma for that fateful day.

Auxiliary Power Unit Fire

The acronym APU means Auxiliary Power Unit or Airborne Power Unit. The reason for describing this same power unit in different ways stems from the feud between the unit's different manufacturers over the right to royalties involving sole producer, and the first manufacturer. It was the change of name by the manufacturer that settled the mess after protracted legal actions.

In flight execution, any fire incident is under the emergency category of airplane hazards. The APU is a self-contained gas turbine engine installed in the tail of the B737 airplane. The unit supplies bleed air that may be used for air conditioning and for the airplane's engine start. It also has an AC electrical generator which is used generally for the airplane's electrical needs before the engines get started. On ground, the unserviceability of the APU, coupled with non-availability of a ground air cooling cart, is what causes that unbearable hot and stuffy cabin before the airplane engines are started. This condition in a tropical climate is quite disastrous. I must say that the fare-paying passenger's aspersion under this harsh condition is similar to that of the crew. One must remember that the crew members are human too. Since APU fire in nature is classified as an emergency, the procedure in containing the fire is spontaneously carried out by recalling the itemised procedure in sequence and executing the actions by memory. The procedure for extinguishing an APU fire is pulling and rotating the APU fire warning switch located at the aft electronic panel in the cockpit. The switch is held for one second in the rotated direction. On the completion of this memory action, the PF calls for the APU-fire checklist. The rest of the procedure involves verifying the right execution of the memory actions and, after completing the rest of the read-and-do items, the PNF calls the checklist complete.

Asymmetrical Trailing Edge Devices

The trailing edge devices on the B737 airplane are the flight and ground spoilers located on the upper surface of each wing. The flight spoilers aid the roll effect of the aileron when the airplane is airborne. The spoiler deployment is activated by the wing ailerons through the pilot control wheel movement. A passenger sitting in the cabin (if able to see from a sitting position) would notice that, when the airplane is in the turn, some panels or surfaces above the wing structure are raised on the down wing, i.e. if the airplane is turning to the right then the right wing will be the down wing, and these spoiler surfaces on the wing will be in the raised position. There are two flight spoilers located on each wing of the B737 airplane. If for any reason an asymmetrical condition occurs in the spoiler arrangement it may cause undesirable roll oscillation to the airplane. This asymmetrical condition is considered an abnormal condition, so the use of the appropriate checklist procedure would put the situation under reasonable control to the end of the flight. The checklist for this is a read-and-do procedure.

The three manoeuvres described here are amongst the numerous manoeuvres reflected on the inset sketch of the simulator format. The main objective of flight simulation is for the pilot to form the habit of being able to easily make the transition from a normal flight to the otherwise smoothly. In real life flight execution, when things go wrong they do so without prior notification, and it is assumed that the natural human concern with self-preservation tends to lead to panic or fear. Familiarity with simulated situations helps to reduce this human handicap to the minimum possible. Emphasis on practice and positive result from flight simulation came to be the accepted pre-emptive training measure to mitigate the consequences of any disastrous event that may be encountered during flight execution. Flight simulation became an important capstone in flight crew training. It is common knowledge among pilots all over the world that consistent satisfactory performance during flight simulation is a form of professional clout. This is because the simulator training not only makes one adept, but helps to raise self-confidence in the crew to an appreciable level. If any emergency occurs, panic is minimal. My belief is that no fine-spun and skilled pilot is worth a tinker's dam if after undergoing a course of simulator training he cannot hold up in the stress of a real emergency situation during flight execution.

The encouraging counsel I got from my partner made me quash completely the thought of course abdication. We now reopened for the third lesson and my friend just held that airplane during the engine out manoeuvre to the extent that the instructor had to get up from his console station to actually visualise that the engine really failed as per what he had set in the computer console. I didn't get to practise the manoeuvre until the fourth lesson and, to the surprise of us all, I just did not crash. It is there on the grading column of the simulator sketch. So the training went on till the 29th of August, 1981, when I went and passed my simulator check. I then went on for the airplane training and finished on the 9th of September, 1981.

United Airlines issued us with prescriptions of "technical elixir" for the operation of the B737 airplane. Then it was home, sweet home.

Flying the B737 as a First Officer

Before I started operations on the B737 airplane, I had to go through another base training on the airplane in Lagos. It had something to do with the unwillingness of the Nigerian Civil Aviation to accept the United Airline Ltd training syllabus. Well, eventually we did the training and got the Federal CAA endorsement and anon, I got on with the line indoctrination training for the airplane. After seventy-seven hours of training, I passed the route check and started operating as a substantive first officer (F/O) on the 31st of May, 1982. And would you believe it, my simulator partner flew and did his route check under me!

I flew as F/O on this craft for a total of 1,700 from the 13th of August 1981 to the 18th of November 1984. For the few years I operated the airplane, I sure went through a torrent of events. I shall only relate a few essential ones. During this period, events like landing gear malfunction, blowing three tyres, and, lastly, the remote case of our losing all compass instruments (except the standby), were the encounters I had before I went through the politically remote case of my "one-day military draft".

Blowing the Tyres

On the 7th of April, 1983, we were operating the Nigeria Airways scheduled service WT 470 routing Lagos–Abuja–Jos–Lagos. The day was bright, cloudless and sunny. It was the kind of day that any pilot would love to fly. On a day like this, the pilot is very happy, while the farmer innocently praying for rain is cursed by the pilot. It was a midday coach service with the first stop in Abuja, the capital city of Nigeria. The trip from block to block, i.e. from parking point in Lagos to parking point in Abuja, in an ideal situation is a fifty-minute trip. It was a few minutes after midday when we took off. Ground temperature gathered from the cumulative weather briefing from all our destination fields was an average of 33 degrees Celsius. The trip to Abuja was quite smooth and uneventful. As expected, we were parked in Abuja after fifty minutes of leaving the parking ramp in Lagos. Although I believe that time is essential to revenue making in airlines, I also think that a professional should always balance the money-making objective with the ethical demands of his profession. And the most important demand in aviation circles is safety. If this is not taken into consideration, the pilot, in working hard to satisfy his company, thereby securing a place in his company's hall of fame, may eventually find himself in his profession's hall of shame.

In Abuja that hot afternoon (ground temperature was 37 degrees Celsius) we spent the optimum turnaround time and continued our routing to Jos. Flight time to Jos was eighteen minutes, and we made it on schedule. Jos ground temperature was 33 degrees Celsius. I had the feeling that we would be forced to spend the night in Jos if care was not taken. I even told the captain that something should be done about the hot weather operation since the trip between Abuja and Jos was a short one. It was the captain's prerogative to decide, so he only listened to what I had to say and said, "Thank you." We got to Jos all right and the captain smoothly landed the airplane. He then applied the brakes, slowed down, turned off the runway and parked the airplane for Jos passengers to disembark.

As I went down to conduct the transit check around the aircraft, I noticed smoke issuing from one of the airplanes tyres. Getting back to the cockpit, I informed the captain of my observation and told him to give it urgent attention. To satisfy my curiosity, I followed him back down. As soon as we got down, we could see that two tyres were flat already, and a third one went down a minute later. It was an embarrassing sight. The passengers

(I did not know that the captain had ordered passenger boarding to Lagos) were already queuing up, while the captain stood transfixed at the wheel-well bay. I went back into the cockpit to wait for him. Remember I had earlier anticipated something going wrong, so this did not come as a surprise to me. The simple reason was that I knew this was a typical hot weather operation and we had one short leg (Abuja–Jos) sandwiched in our routing, so I expected us to do some brake cooling which could be achieved either on the ground or while airborne. Why the captain never bothered about this is still a mystery to me. Since the moment we left Lagos, the heat absorbed by the wheel brakes had been cumulative, so if the crew did not find a way of dissipating this heat, the end result would be either of two things: a wheel-well fire or the situation in which we now found ourselves. The wheel well is that hollow bay into which the landing gear module as a whole retracts after take-off. If the temperature inside this well gets too hot, it triggers a red light and an alarm bell in the cockpit. In such a situation, the light signals that there is a fire in the wheel-well bay. This is an emergency situation, so the crew's response should be spontaneous. All initial actions would then be carried out by memory as the pilot flying calls for the wheel-well fire checklist.

The only sad thing about what happened in Jos that afternoon, apart from the undesirable fact of revenue loss, was the emotional current that flowed in the cockpit on the arrival of the captain. *He just plainly wept.* That really got to me. I was earlier on planning to scold him politely for getting us in this avoidable setback, but those sobs of his just got me fully debilitated. What happened next is history.

The Landing Gear Event

In airplane operations, every detail or professional knowledge, no matter how small, superfluous, unbelievable or bizarre, should always be kept at the back of the pilot's mind. This is because there comes a time in his career when a rather trivial piece of information may save him and everybody else.

It was another day at work and of course it was business as usual. The service WT 542 was an afternoon departure from

Lagos to Kano, Maiduguri, then back to Kano, and finally back to Lagos. It was another beautiful day in terms of the weather, and in terms of the captain as well (because it could be a big drag flying with some captains sometimes, just as some captains too often find their co-pilots boring). We departed Lagos on schedule. Indeed, we departed all stations on schedule, and at last we began the final leg from Kano back to Lagos. The equipment was one of the oldest in the fleet, but quite a beautiful airplane to handle from a pilot's point of view. A few minutes after we passed Bida (a town in the middle belt of the country close to the River Niger) the sun dipped below the horizon and darkness set in. We soon got in contact with the Lagos approach air traffic control and, later, we were cleared to descend into Lagos. It was still business as usual until we got on the final approach path for runway 19L in Lagos. Then the captain called for gear extension and the final-landing checklist. While reading the checklist items and making sure that things were in order, I suddenly noticed that there was a red light on the landing gear nose warning light panel instead of the expected green light. At this phase of the flight, I as the PNF had already told the Lagos approach ATS unit that we had left the Lima Golf (LG) facility and that we had the runway in sight. We were cleared to continue with Lagos tower for further landing instructions. Unfortunately, that was not to be.

I established contact with Lagos tower, informed them that we had problems with our landing gear, and asked for clearance to go back to the LG facility and start a hold as published so that we could sort out our abnormal situation with a promise to call back as soon as we had got the problem sorted out. We were given clearance accordingly, and into the hold we went. The captain was doing the flying, so he called out for the manual-gear-extension checklist. Before I go on, I must state here that the nose gear red light warning meant that the nose gear was not extended at all, or it was extended but not well locked in the down position, thereby making it unsafe for landing. Well, in flight execution, there is always an alternative to any of the airplane systems. In this case, our first option was to now try a manual extension of the gear. We went through this procedure in accordance with the checklist, but the problem remained the same.

The next logical and recommended procedure is one that any pilot would try to avoid if he could. It is landing the airplane with the rest of the extended gear. This is a partial gear landing situation, and also a toss-up. Now this is where the captain has to apply his wealth of experience so as to save the situation. The captain that evening did just that. How did he do it? Well, the whole thing went like this. As part of the manual gear extension procedure, it was the duty of the PNF to go and visually check through window or gear view windows, located at different stations in the airplane, and verify continuity in the gear down and locked red line from these viewers. The nose gear viewer is in the cockpit just aft of the cockpit's control stand on the cockpit floor. Now the problem we had was with the nose wheel, and the captain applied his wealth of experience after a synthesis of valid and very logical reasons. He knew the airplane was an old one (i.e. she might be prone to false warnings, especially as it was an electrical type fault). And, because he believed that the fault was electrical, he made sure that I did a visual check not only on the nose gear but on the rest of the landing gear module. Before I left my station to commence the main wheel gear check, we requested to fly over Lagos tower at an altitude of 2,000 ft so that the tower hand could also tell us the real configuration of the landing gear. After we did this, we got a positive response from the tower hand. So far, what was going on was known only to us, the cabin crew, and the ATC unit. And it had been going on for the past twenty minutes or so.

I entered the cabin in order to perform the visual check on the main wheel gears through the viewers located in the cabin just three seats aft of the cabin emergency window exit. This was when I had to face the public for the first time in my life while airborne, and also in an abnormal situation like this. Before I relate my encounter with the passengers who, naturally as earthlings, had to obey the laws of homogenesis involving self-preservation and panic, I shall first relate a story told by an instructor of mine, Mr Ron Frink of the Sierra Academy of Aeronautics, when I was in the USA, undergoing my flight engineering course on the B727 turbojet. On the last day of the ground school phase of the course the instructor told us that after graduation, and when actively employed as flight engineers, we should not do what a certain flight engineer did on a European passenger carrier airline flight from Tokyo, Japan to the UK. The flight engineer left his station during taxiing for take-off with permission from the captain to go and attend to his physiological needs. He dashed through the cabin for the rear toilet in order to get back in time before the airplane reached the take-off position. Well, little did he realise that he had just made history by this speed of his. How? Well, while he was dashing through the cabin like a bat out of hell, there were these two well-travelled passengers who recognised the rank he was wearing and also were quite conversant with the role played by any crew wearing that rank in the cockpit. So what did they do? They looked at each other and after a very brief dialogue, arrived at the wrong conclusion that something bad was going on and they certainly weren't going to be any part of it. Fortunately for them, they were seated at the emergency over-wing exit window. So they quickly opened the exit, made a break for it to the wings and hung on there waiting for the craft to come to a stop so that they could jump down and make their final escape.

While they were dashing through the left over-wing exit, of course, other passengers who did not know the reason for their action followed too. The other passengers on the right side of the airplane's cabin opened the window in the stampede, and off they went too for the wings. The cockpit crew on their part were entirely oblivious of the situation in the cabin, and in the course of carrying out their duties requested take-off clearance from the control tower who responded by asking the captain to actually confirm if they were ready for take-off because, in their own opinion, if they could just look over their wings, they would know for a fact that they were not near ready for any take-off. And when the captain looked, he just couldn't believe what he saw! Passengers were now all over the airplane wings. The rest is better left imagined.

Now, as I opened the cockpit door to enter the cabin, these were the thoughts that flooded my mind. A passenger in the front row of seats touched my hand and asked: "First Officer, is there something wrong?"

I smiled broadly, and told him: "No." He wasn't quite convinced, because as I walked away from him with as much composure as I could manage, I overheard him asking the cabin staff how come we had not landed yet. Especially because, following normal procedure, the cabin staff had announced as soon as they saw the gear coming down that we would be on the ground shortly, and both the "No smoking" and "Fasten seat belt" signs were on. Going by all these pointers, their making that cabin announcement was quite in order. As I walked towards the location of the main wheel gear viewers, all eyes were on me. That didn't bother me a bit. I was out there to do a job. Also, I wasn't going to induce any iota of fear in these people. As soon as I got to the location I greeted the Alhaji seated in that area in the only Hausa word I knew, smiled broadly and asked him to kindly vacate his seat to let me retrieve an important item that an engineer had left under his seat, which we now needed to be able to land in Lagos so that he could meet his Hajia who by now must be desperately waiting for him. The gentlemen just laughed, shifted his weight and didn't say anything more. I bent forward, looked through the viewer and found everything in order. So I went back to the cockpit and informed the captain, and right away, light or no light, we requested landing clearance. Thank God that for every system the airplane has an alternative litmus or confidence test. In the end, it was a smooth landing, and what a pleasure it was to be back home too!

The bottom line is that when flying an old horse one should expect anything.

And We Lost All Compasses

There is a Yoruba adage that says: "That madman you see wandering around all day long has no destination. There is no provision for his bath, and that is what makes him scruffy and messy. Technically speaking, the madman has lost his mental compass."

The primary navigational instrument for airplanes is the compass. The role it plays in navigation is to give signals to the more sophisticated navigational units installed in most airplanes.

All the other navigational units are tied to the airplane's compass system. Telescopically viewed, the compass is the reference datum for the rest of the navigational units. I have not heard of any airplane yet that flies without a compass unit on board. On the B737, there are three compass units, one on each crew member's instrument panel and one back-up unit called the standby unit. Incidentally, it is to the standby unit that one makes reference when in doubt of the signals from the two other units. With the loss of this vital unit, one becomes like the madman in the Yoruba adage. And the passengers unfortunately become part of the journey to nowhere. Then secondly, the trip to nowhere terminates as soon as the airplane runs out of fuel. And then the law of gravity takes over. So the major difference is that the madman who lost his compass can still survive the law of gravity by virtue of being on the ground. That is probably why he never got worried in the first place the day he lost his compass.

The 14th of March 1983 was a day that most Nigeria Airways pilots enthusiastically looked forward to as far as this particular service, WT 912 was concerned. It was scheduled as a mid-afternoon departure that eventually terminated in Monrovia at 21.00 GMT after flying through stations like Contonou, Lome and Abidjan. It was usually followed by the award night formalities which involved being paid the night stop allowance of $240 and, later, getting in rhythm with whatever form of hospitality the people had to offer. The choice of what and how to entertain yourself was all yours. Due to the poor remuneration of the airline this was one award night all pilots in the fleet looked forward to, and one they would do almost anything not to miss. Well, that is the natural reaction to what money has become. It is these overnight layover trips that pilots generally refer to as the night stop run.

The afternoon of the flight was business as usual, but with a lot of enthusiasm. Our crew composition was three cockpit crew and four cabin staff. I was the bona fide F/O, but, apart from the captain, we had a senior first officer with us who had been recommended for additional line indoctrination training as a corrective measure for not meeting the required proficiency level expected of him as a qualified first officer on the B737 airplane during his last pilgrimage (which pilots in Nigeria Airways make half-yearly) to the simulator facility. In this case, for him to be reinstated to his former status, he would be scheduled for a proficiency check on the airplane after completing fifty mandatory hours of line flight. As far as the date he became first officer on the airplane was concerned, he was way ahead my senior. As I have already highlighted, attaining the required standard in airplane proficiency was an absolute requirement and never an advisory thing. So, as a sign of respect, I vacated my seat for him so he could have real practice by actually handling the airplane, as long as the captain was in agreement. He was, and I occupied the jump seat, or the third crew observer's seat, for quite some time during the trip.

Now I must say that generally in airplane operations, when things are about to go wrong, there are usually prior indicators or pointers to the impending fault. But the harsh truth is, if the crew is not technically conversant with the airplane their technical handicap may prove very disastrous. Well, in our own case, it was during our descent into Abidjan from Lome that we started noticing that the number one compass kept tumbling from time to time. Since we still had two back-ups and this fault was only intermittent, we just made a note of the problem. Usually the custom on the B737 fleet regarding night stop flights is for these flights to be accompanied by at least one airplane maintenance engineer. Ideally, any persons qualified as flight engineers are legal entities to perform the duties of an engineer while airborne. This is the legal crew composition on three-man airplanes like the B747, the DCl0, etc.

On most two-man-crew airplanes the crew workload has been reduced to the barest minimum, and an airborne flight engineer would be a blatant waste of vital manpower. But since it is common knowledge that sometimes a malfunction can occur on an otherwise good and normal instrument, most carriers that recognise the essence of time in passenger operations prefer to have on board a qualified maintenance engineer for most of these two-man crew jets in order to avoid nuisance delays in case of a breakdown during normal passenger flights. So far, this has proved quite effective.

So while airborne, as soon as we got the first signs of this impending malfunction, we called the attention of the maintenance engineer to it. On the ground in Abidjan the engineer probed into the fault and was able to reset the unit. So we continued the trip to our final destination which was Monrovia. It was during our descent into the Robertsfield Airport that the torrent of events that led us into a total state of quandary manifested. The whole stampede started shortly after we had established radio communication with the Robertsfield approach control and later requested for descent clearance into the airport. Suddenly, as we descended through 10,000 ft, both the captain's and the co-pilot's compasses just processed and tumbled. For a second, we thought it was just another transient thing, but we were shocked to find out otherwise. Both units had failed.

It was a very bad experience in the sense that it was completely dark now, and, by fate or something, the VOR facility in Robertsfield was off the air. And we were not even precisely on course before this awful thing happened. The navigational aids at Robertsfield Airport were also unserviceable, and all we had with the airfield was radio contact. It was pitch dark, and I imagined that the shadow of the valley of death couldn't be worse than this. Before the compass failed, we were still circumnavigating this rainstorm cell (a big one too) directly on our flight path to Robertsfield. The captain wanted to avoid the cell because penetrating a rainstorm cell gets the airplane tossed around just the way a common balloon is tossed around when thrown inside water, except that in the case of the airplane human beings also get violently tossed around in the instability of the water-saturated rainstorm cell. Sometimes the turbulence in certain cells may cause danger to the airplane structure and subsequently injury to fare-paying passengers. In avoiding this, the captain had made a heading change of about 40 degrees off course, and we had stayed on this heading for more than nineteen minutes before the compass loss turned the whole trip into a nightmare.

It was a chain of grief from that moment on. All the odds expected of this type of situation were against us. Coincidentally, we were about turning back to intercept the airway or course

MONROVIA, LIBERIA
ROBERTS INTL
ILS Rwy 04
LOC 110.3 SK

ROBERTS Approach **124.5**	
ROBERTS Tower **118.3**	
Ground **121.9**	
Alt Set: MB (IN on req)	Trans level: FL50
Rwy Elev: 1 MB	Trans alt: 3000' (2971')

3000'

MSA
ROB VOR

Apt. Elev 31'

(IAF)

328° 1033'☀

HOLDING OVER
VOR OR MO NDB   ∧591'

•380'

300'

044°
3000

•184'

ROBERTS
372 MO   ☀971'

301°

1500 No PT
10 DME Arc

162'

110°   (IAF)

ROBERTS
263 FR   160'

MM

ROBERTS
D **113.8 ROB**

224°

151°

235°

044°

179°

OM

3000

359°

ILS
044° 110.3 SK

213°

1500 No PT
10 DME Arc

GL(D)-42

06-20   06-10   18-30   18-20

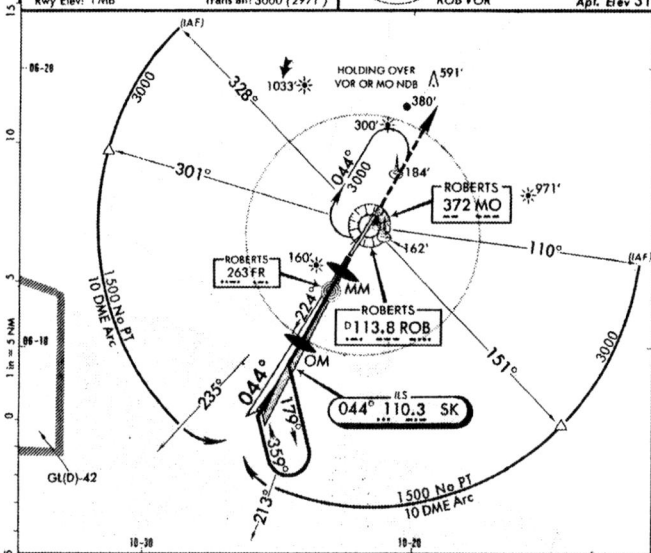

VFR traffic along coastline up to 500 ft MSL.

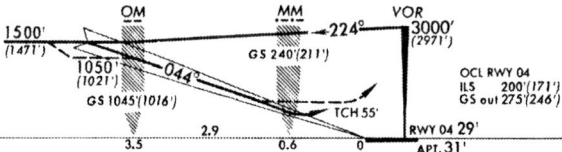

OM   MM   VOR
1500'   224°   3000'
(1471')   (2971')

1050'
(1021')   044°

GS 240'(211')

OCL RWY 04
ILS   200'(171')
GS out 275'(246')

GS 1045'(1016')

TCH 55'

RWY 04 29'

3.5   2.9   0.6   0   APT. 31'

MISSED APPROACH: Climb STRAIGHT AHEAD to 1500' (1471') and contact ATC.

	STRAIGHT-IN LANDING RWY 04				
	ILS			LOC (GS out)	
	DH 229' (200')		DH 279' (250')	MDA 280' (251')	
	FULL	ALS out	MM out	MM out	ALS out
A					
B	800m	1200m	800m	800m	1600m
C					
D			1200m	1200m	1600m

Gnd speed-Kts	70	90	100	120	140	160
GS 2.55°	321	413	458	550	642	733
OM to MAP 3.5	3:00	2:20	2:06	1:45	1:30	1:19

CHANGES: Obst.

NOT DRAWN TO SCALE

toward Robertsfield when this incident occurred. The captain was the PF and muttering in his Rausa dialect, he naturally reached out and extended the airplane's standby compass. On the B737-200 airplane the standby compass is retracted and folded out of view at the upper windshield panel location in the cockpit since it is meant for the use of both pilots in monitoring without any hindrance to their forward field of vision. The unit's location is indeed in the most central position in the cockpit.

Basically, the standby compass is quite vacillating in behaviour. It is reminiscent of the common compass unit that most avid navigators (whether pilots or not) can usually pick up from any book store or street vendor. Let us take for example the common ones seen in some automobiles. If one is quite observant, when a car negotiates a turn, one notices that the unit dances round and round for a period before it finally settles at a particular heading. In an airplane, this period would make the cockpit crew quite unsettled because of the speed at which a jet is travelling.

As a career pilot, using the standby compass unit for navigation requires a wealth of knowledge that one probably practised last while in initial flight training school. The remoteness of a situation like this in career flying is what makes the whole idea of using the unit very undesirable.

Most airlines operate a communication arrangement that involves a two-way dialogue between the captain and his assistants. This is because of the belief that as long as flight crews maintain continuity in communication during all phases of flight execution, in the event of an unexpected occurrence of incapacitation relating to a crew member, detection of this potentially disastrous condition by the other crew members is quite prompt.

During the short dialogue between my senior colleague (occupying my seat) and the captain, the former gave up all hope, turned around to me and said, "Ty, why don't you just have back your seat? I don't like what is going on one bit." He then vacated the seat and surprised us further by leaving the cockpit! To me, his conduct was quite disappointing, unprofessional and bad for morale. Till today, I still do not want to believe that that chap ever did this. (Today he is a captain with a general aviation outfit.)

Well, I took my seat after he vacated it. Surprisingly enough, as soon as I settled down in my seat I became appreciative of his absence from the cockpit. From his rather weird conduct, I believed he would have been a nuisance in the cockpit if he had stayed any longer, which of course would have made the whole situation more unbearable for us. Since the cell circumvention took us to the right of our course, the captain logically turned towards the left, and past our course heading, thereby achieving a certain degree of course interception. This was a sound professional judgement. But the big question was, how would we know when course interception had been achieved? Meanwhile, while the captain and I were pondering this, we were cleared further down to 3,000 ft by Robertsfield approach, and were to continue further radio communication with the tower on frequency 118.3 MHz. It was a continuous descent all through to 3,000 ft, but destination-wise our heading was by no means certain. On 3,000 ft altitude, we should, by our estimation, be within a 21-mile radius of Robertsfield Airport if we had been on course and hadn't done any circumnavigating. Well, the only thing that the 3,000 ft altitude made clear to us was the fact that we were over the ocean, and of course this meant we were completely lost and widely off course. As PNF, I established contact with Robertsfield tower and told them we were levelled at 3,000 ft. The tower just cleared us for Robertsfield ILS (Instrument Landing System) approach for runway 04 and requested our revised estimates for Robertsfield, which alarmingly was now twelve minutes out. We really didn't have any answer to that request, so we just told the tower to stand by on that, and we asked whether Robertsfield VOR was serviceable. To our surprise, the tower man's response was in the affirmative, which meant the VOR was operational and in the air. Well, this only meant then that we were too far away and out of range of the VOR's signal reception. From the Jeppesen let-down chart for the ILS approach runway 04 for Robertsfield Airport, the letter "D" in the VOR facility rectangular box meant that the facility was co-located with the distance measuring equipment (DME). Unfortunately too, though we had the VOR tuned, the DME window on the instrument panel was blank, which meant the airborne, or the ground facility unit, or both, were unserviceable. One thing I will never forget about this flight is the action the captain took as soon as I told him we had been cleared for the Robertsfield ILS 04 approach. He held his heading (on the standby compass) for a few seconds more, and then out of the blue he gave a command that I should tune the frequency on my navigation box. As soon as I did this, the azimuth vertical bar for the ILS instrument drifted and hung to the furthest side of the circular instrument unit, and before I knew it the captain just turned the airplane's heading towards the ILS azimuth bar. Well, at least he did something, but the instrument panel was showing a red flag, which meant the instrument was not reliable yet, both in azimuth (or course) guidance and the electronic glide path as well. Well, the captain held this heading and also the 3,000 ft altitude and we kept flying. And all of a sudden, "eureka", the VOR DME came on and reflected 99 nautical miles and almost at abeam position of Robertsfield airfield. The captain then turned the airplane until the DME distance started reducing, which confirmed without any doubt now our flying somewhere towards Monrovia at least. About eight minutes later, we saw the shoreline and also some lights on the ground which showed at least that we were around some inhabited community. It was some relief when we got closer and realised that it was the small village around Robertsfield airport called Smell No Taste. And when we went closer still, we just saw the runway ahead of us. The rest is now history, but we made it. Somehow, to this day I still cannot figure out properly how we did it.

The event had completely spoilt the expectant and happy mood of the award night. As far as we were concerned, we just couldn't wait to run away from that airplane. When the captain finally parked he said something that I would never forget. This was over dinner at the hotel later in the evening. He said to me: "Ty, I have decided to get back to Lagos tomorrow by ship. As for the rest of you guys, it's up to you what you want to do."

For him, as far as that particular airplane was concerned, we should just forget that he was the captain that had brought her that far. So he asked me where he could find the telephone number for a passenger shipping line in Liberia. Well, I really got thrown, and felt sorry all through for the captain. But I did not see the rationale in his decision. For me, it was a case of if anything could go wrong while flying an airplane then it would go wrong, so I didn't see the point of the big turn-off in the captain. It was years later when I became a captain myself that I clearly got to understand his line of thinking when he said he would not fly that plane any longer. I remember ignorantly telling him that though his decision to go back to Lagos by ship was quite understandable, he should remember that ships were also compass-steered. So the whole situation was still a toss-up. I shall explain in detail the folly of my misunderstanding the captain's thinking later on under the sub-heading "The Making of a Captain".

Contrary to the captain's desire to go by ship back to Lagos, the rescue team of engineers from Lagos arrived, and after working into the following day they got the problem rectified. After a few minutes of test-flying the airplane, the captain agreed to fly it back to Lagos. But this time with a condition: the flight was strictly to be without passengers on board. Just the crew.

I usually refer to this event as the "Smell No Taste Debacle". Why? Because it was the settlement with this name that gave us the assurance that we had arrived at the airport vicinity. Though the name of this village sounded a bit weird to me, on enquiry from one of the inhabitants I found out that the name came to be during Liberia's colonial days. The American colonial masters had their own clan around Robertsfield Airfield. The small clan of Americans then cooked very aromatic meals, which most times made the villagers hang around the boundary between the American and African sections of the village to smell the appetising aroma of the cooking. Of course, they never tasted any part of it. So, the village came to be known as Smell No Taste after the Americans left. I pray that this village will still remain after the power struggle between Mr Charles Taylor and the rest of the Liberian gold-diggers is over.

One-Day Military Draft as Pawns in the Military Chess Game

The country was not on the verge of war, and it was peace time globally around the world, so the 1st of January 1984 was like any normal New Year's Day. It was a relatively cold harmattan morning. I had a girlfriend who had spent the previous night with me since the rostered schedule indicated the 1st of January as my off-day. The previous night I had had dinner with my girlfriend and we went home to continue the New Year vigil by watching some video films before we finally turned in. Since it was a public holiday, some TV stations were on air for twenty-four hours. I was still in a deep slumber when my girlfriend shook me up frantically to witness the special New Year TV broadcast, which I remember was not one of the television items of programmes read to us the previous night. That must have been the reason for my girlfriend's unnecessary excitement, I thought, as I looked to see what it was all about. There was music from the TV but what that form of music usually signalled was what got me fully awake. It was martial music. It was then followed by a public announcement of the reason for the playing of martial music. I was now fully alert. Then I saw the person making the announcement. He was wearing full military uniform. I wondered who he could be until he introduced himself as Brigadier Sanni Abacha. The announcement was repeated intermittently for almost ten hours. I just told my girlfriend "thank you" and went back to sleep. Little did I know that a few hours later, I would be playing a faceless backup role as a chorus singer to that music.

At about 10.00 a.m. that morning, my girlfriend woke me up, but she was doing this for the second time! Before I could say something, she just said to me, "Ty! You have a visitor." Well, she knew pretty well that the penalty for the offence she had committed twice was sexual deprivation for at least six days. I walked out of my bedroom to see a Nigerian Airways dispatcher friend of mine looking worried and very tired, apparently from lack of sleep. We exchanged greetings and he informed me verbally that I was required for a flight. What a joke! I said to myself. It was the first day of the month, agreed, but it certainly wasn't the month of April. Both the radio and television were on. Well, to set my thought right, I asked the dispatcher to join me if he liked to listen to music or watch the TV. I also told him to forget the idea of my coming to work. He just smiled nervously and said, "Ty, the flight you're required for is in connection with this programme. If you don't believe me, please look out of your window." I looked out of the window for a while, but nothing unusual was out there. I saw an Airways van and the rest of the buildings on the close. Looking more closely I noticed that the passengers in the van were dressed in the uniform of the Nigerian Air Force.

There were three of them with the driver. I turned back inside and asked the dispatcher what was going on, and he told me how they had been in the custody of these guys since 3.00 a.m. I asked him, "Why me?" I was off duty according to the roster, and there were thirty other co-pilots he could have gone to.

He just replied "Ty, I was instructed by the chief pilot to get you."

"Why?"

"I don't know."

Well, no further questions. I did not need any special intellect to interpret the presence of unusual government officials. I just told him, OK, I would be at the airport in the next hour. But he stood there, not moving. I asked him what was going on and he replied, "Sir, I was instructed to wait for you till you were ready and then bring you along." He waited while I got ready. Thirty minutes later, we were on our way to the airport.

The drive to the airport was quite interesting. The presence of the military was evident everywhere. There were road blocks. For us there was no problem. The military guys in the van carried on them the pass we needed. The street was almost desolate. Things looked too spooky and eerie for the first day of the year. Eventually we got to the airport. The whole of the dispatch office was a beehive of activity. As I got off the van, the first riddle was solved.

My very good friend, mentor, and probably the most intelligent captain I had flown with as a first officer, came up to me and informed me that we were to fly to Jos as soon as the airplane was ready. Then we walked off to the crew restroom. All through the drive to the airport, I had wondered who could have chosen me to fly on a day like this. I now knew. My captain friend had a preference for me whenever it came to flying. He loved flying with me and I loved flying with him too. He was probably the only captain I flew with throughout my co-pilot career who I really enjoyed flying with. And having got airborne with him, I never wanted the flight to end. His trade secret? Cockpit management and cruise entertainment. The captain was an ex-air force officer, and he loved roses.

The crew restroom was something else. All other cockpit crew members who reported that day, including me, became celebrities. Why? Imagine that while waiting for the aircraft, the chief pilot asked us what we would like to eat, drove to the catering office himself for it, came back, and did the serving himself! Not only that, the director of flight operation came in later to ask us if we wanted anything else. What was going on? Was this stardom, or kamikaze final rites? Well, so far, I was enjoying every bit of it.

At about 12.30 GMT, my captain sent for me to get on the way. My role was strictly to do my duties. He didn't even call me for dispatch crew briefing. He just said, "Yoruba, let's go. Right now we are going to Jos." We then walked towards the Nigeria Airways B737 number 5N-ANW with four cabin attendants sauntering after us. During our short walk to the airplane I asked the captain what the weather was like in Jos knowing how hazy it was in Lagos. He looked at me for a moment before he said, "It should be okay." There and then I knew this was no more a flight. It was a mission. It was compulsory. But this was not the Nigerian Air Force. This was Nigeria Airways. We were not into missions, but civil passenger services. For him, everything was in order. His air force orientation was being revisited. It must have been fun for him. As for me, I was in a total quandary. For today and for this flight, I ceased to be a civilian. No bill of rights. No laws just orders. Too bad! There was no getting out of it, so the best thing to do was to make the best of the flight.

We did our external checks and boarded the airplane. Apart from the cabin attendants and one engineer, we had only three military personnel as passengers. One of them, a colonel, sat with us in the cockpit. Meanwhile, all borders were closed and a curfew was on. But the ATC guys were waiting for us to call for start-up. Well, we did, and got the clearance. Within ten minutes we were airborne. We were the only airplane airborne so far that day. The whole airspace was quiet. We seemed to be the only airplane station communicating with all the en route ATC units all the way to Jos. I turned my HP box to the BBC, and of course the Nigerian event was hot news. After about two minutes, I turned the box off. Later on, I got contact with Jos tower and requested the weather. As I had guessed, it was below landing minimums. I didn't need to inform the captain. He was listening out and flying the airplane. As we got descent clearance into Jos, the military personnel in the cockpit told me to inform the Jos ATC unit to get in touch with the military in respect of our arrival time and so on. This I did.

At Jos, the airport environment was the same – more military cast, more vehicles, then a small group of gentlemen dressed in mufti but looking as serious as military men. They were dressed in "Babanriga" (gowns) and formed a small circle on the tarmac. They were waiting for our airplane to come to a stop. As soon as we did, the captain and the colonel left to talk to these people. I got down too to do my job, the external walk around the airplane. While I was doing this, a middle-aged chap came up to me and introduced himself in the rank of a military general. He then inquired what the events were like in Lagos. To tell the truth, I just could not figure out the kind of answer he expected from me, but I had to give him one. So I told him how my girlfriend had woken me up in the morning to watch the TV broadcast of the military man who introduced himself as Brigadier Abacha and that the programme content was his speech on better leadership for the country. "Sir, that's all I know," I said. The general thanked me and, while he was walking away from me, he complained quietly that he was on leave and just couldn't figure out why his presence was required in Lagos. Since it was a soliloquy, I just continued my walk-around duty.

We spent almost two hours waiting to get the full gathering of the people whose names the colonel had. In the end, the gentlemen were all gathered. The head of the team (a two-star general) was probably in his late forties, and was quite alert, calm and collected in his conduct. He was of average height, very dark, slim and had a sprinkle of grey hair on his head. He was clearly in charge. Later on during our return trip, the captain informed me that the personality was the longest-serving two-star general in the Nigerian army then. It was no surprise then that he was made the first military joint chief of staff in free Africa. I must say the man radiated confidence in the way he gave out orders. He once joined us in the cockpit to make use of our communication equipment, and after getting his message across to wherever he was transmitting to he thanked us and told us our next destination was now Kaduna. We could see he was clearly in charge. He left our cockpit and went back to the cabin. A few minutes later, we took off for Kaduna. The Jos to Kaduna trip took under thirty minutes. On board already were four military generals and some other military officers with their families.

At Kaduna Airport, things were not as peaceful as they were in Jos. In Jos, military guys and their tanks were all over the place but the tanks were stationary. In Kaduna this was not so. The military presence was quite scary. The population was larger, they were dressed in battle gear. What made things worse for me was the fact that here, all those weapons of death and destruction were moving around the whole airport, the tarmac, the runway, the taxi-way, etc. I concluded that this must be the launching pad or site for the production of this movie. A lot of the directing must have taken place here. We spent quite a long, and for me, unsettling period of time here. While we were parked in Kaduna, the general in control from Jos came to the cockpit once again and informed us that while he was on the radio box, he would appreciate our total absence from the cockpit. We vacated the cockpit immediately. I sat in the cabin, and just didn't feel like going down to the tarmac, duty or no duty. All along, I had monomaniacally taken relish in this movie, but now, I was more than ready to turn the set off. While we were in the cabin, the captain read this on my face but kept quiet. From the cabin, I could see exchanges of emotions, argument, coupled with speculative looks and conduct. I just couldn't wait to get out of there. I also prayed that our next destination with orders from the general would be Lagos. As far as I was concerned, this was no more the Kaduna airport I had flown into times without number with passengers queuing peacefully to embark the airplane. The airport was now a military base, and one under a crisis too. As fate would have it, boarding commenced. The general allowed us back into the cockpit and thanked us once again. One thing I liked about this gentleman was that he surely knew how to relate to civilians. His tone was so soothing that it quashed any negative thought that could start to form in one's mind. Thank God, part of his cockpit handover courtesy included our destination, which was Lagos. In the end, everybody that had to be on board was now in the cabin. We got the airplane's door closed and then requested start-up clearance.

As usual, we got cleared, and after starting both engines, we taxied as cleared towards Kaduna runway 23 holding point for take-off. All communications with ATC were unconventional. The controller gave us clearance to line up and wait on the runway for final take-off clearance. As we lined up on the runway, two military tanks suddenly drove out from nowhere and lined up head-on with us, their tank nozzles pointed at us. I took one look at the captain, then the captain shifted the look (or blame) to the military officer in the cockpit with us.

The general then looked out and simultaneously grabbed the captain's microphone and called Kaduna tower with orders for Kaduna tower to contact the military tower in Kaduna. After about four minutes of transmission he returned the microphone to the captain. I sat there looking. Needless to say, all sorts of thoughts raced through my mind. Well, after about ten minutes that seemed an eternity to me, the tanks turned around and revved off the runway. So we too revved off as fast as we could, and got airborne.

As soon as we arrived in Lagos, the general came up to us in the cockpit and greeted us for the last time. Before he finally left, he left me with one of his complementary cards. Whoa! I could not wait to get out of the airplane. As soon as I did, I told the captain, "Next time, captain, *please don't remember me in hell*." This sure wasn't a day's job. For three days I was so disorganised. I sent word that I wasn't coming to work. Thank God the generals were in full control. It would have been disastrous if they hadn't got their act together.

This was my last interesting experience as a first officer on the B737 before I went on to fly the airbus (A310). Flying the Airbus as a first officer is what I have called "the good life" in the next chapter.

Airbus 310 Airplane. Courtesy: Nigeria Airways

The Good Life

Flying the A310 as first officer (F/O) was, in my own career opinion, the good life as far as flying went. This transition from the societal poverty envelope to this status started from the onset of the transition training for the airplane itself. Before the transition training, my career as a pilot had been strictly confined to the route web of the airline as it related to the equipment and the fleets I had served on. My schedule on the fleets I had earlier served on (i.e. F27 and B737) confined me mostly to the company's local routes and the West/East African coasts. This structure formed a larger percentage of the company's route network. Personally, as a career pilot, I had always looked forward to the day I would be operating on the company's continental routes. Flying the airbus made this dream come true at last.

The aspiration of passenger carrier pilots in this regard is a universal thing. Being able to leave home for work and become part of an entirely different community, culture and society initially seems to be a common ambition for pilots. Unfortunately, flying these routes becomes a routine and, with the length of time spent airborne during these flights, the whole thing gradually becomes as boring as trying to walk the Mojave desert. So, before it gets boring, the wise crew member makes the best of the euphoric period. The A310 is a medium-range airplane, i.e. it has an endurance of about nine hours of which any trip within six and a half hours is considered safe, as far as fuel regulations from the governing aviation authorities all over the world go. It is also categorised under the wide-bodied airplane group. It has a passenger seating capacity of between 235 and 300, depending on the preference of the customer's order and specification, the customer here being the airline of course.

At the time I did my transition course for the airplane, it was the most technologically advanced jet airliner. This was because it was the first commercial airplane installed with Cathode Ray

Tube (CRT) screens along with computerised software materials whose TV-like screen gradually replaced the conventional clock-like airplane cockpit instrumentation. Today, most jet airplane cockpits are fashioned after this CRT concept. As I have always mentioned, the month of January is the most eventful in my life and career. I got certified as a pioneer crew member with Nigeria Airways on the A310 airplane towards the end of January 1985.

The month of January has remained the most peaceful in my life. I got married two days before the month of January, and my wife and I had our first son, Olushegun, on the 27th of January 1989.

Getting to fly the airbus finally gave me the chance to correct the one wrong attitude most people in our society, educated and uneducated alike, usually exhibit. Most times at social functions, when people get introduced, their professional tags form part of the introduction. The next routine question that usually came after the formal exchange of greetings was when next you would be flying out to London or New York. Once you had been introduced as a pilot, this question was bound to be asked. After uncountable experiences in this line, I was forced to conclude that, ordinarily, most people think that for a pilot, flying all over the world is the normal thing. I must mention here that this belief, though true for some airlines, is generally wrong. Most times it takes climbing the professional ladder before one gets to that point. For me, it took from 1979 to 1984 before I finally got there. Coincidentally, it was the peak of Jimmy Johnson's jingo of "London today, Milan tomorrow" etc. Incidentally, that was precisely what we were doing, and I had three and a half years of it myself.

Flying out to the western world makes life a fantasy for Third World pilots. This is because, suddenly, purchasing western materials becomes the essence of living. Getting out of one's Third World home country becomes so welcome, and after some time it takes a great effort to readjust to the home life. This was my experience when I left the A310 fleet.

The purchase of the A310 airplane by Nigeria Airways made news both locally and internationally. On the local scene, it turned out to be the ruling civilian government's big achievement. Internationally, Nigeria Airways turned out to be one of the manufacturer's pioneer customers. The final order for four of these airplanes was a big business both for the manufacturers and the Nigerian government. The first of the airplanes was flown into Nigeria by the pair of Captain Olu-Lawal and Senior First Officer (SF/O) Araba, while the second one was flown in by Captain Machunga and SF/O Caulcrick. So big was the event that they were met on arrival by dance troupes, government officials, and of course the innocent public and passers-by who could only enjoy the event by watching through the Murtala Mohammed Airport fences. The pilots who flew in the two airplanes with all the fanfare and ceremony were engrossed in the festivities.

Everything about the A310, including the transition training, was unique. During the transition training in Tolouse, France (this happened to be the manufacturer's base for flight crew training), the PLATO facility was revisited. Only this time the PLATO menu incorporated the topics, with the technical details, for all the different systems installed in the airplane. In short, the ground school was absolutely another PLATO affair. It was only the writing of the final ground school examination that divorced us from PLATO. For me, it sure was an exciting way to start a course. Familiarity with the PLATO which I earlier used for my training was not only an edge but an asset too. The course programme was another jet airplane transition course, except for the technological deviation of the cockpit instruments. The entire flight crew was trained for the line indoctrination by the manufacturers because the airplane was new in the market and Nigeria Airways was one of the launch customers. Since the airplane was entirely new, no indigenous hand (Nigerian) was qualified yet then to conduct the line training.

The opportunity of being trained by the airplane manufacturer's instructors was a very educating experience. This concept is a customary thing among all airplane manufacturers. Since the manufacturer's standard and procedure are legally authoritative, I did a line flight training period of twenty-five hours (contrary to the company's policy of 100 hours LIT) before I got through the check flight that established and confirmed my status as a substantive F/O on the A310.

It was then that the fantasy and transient good life started. A typical A310 crew member is a very viable hand in any airline carrier outfit. The A310 airplane is both a short- and a medium-range airplane with the performance so advanced and flexible. Although the airplane is categorised as a wide-bodied craft, her advanced technology makes it possible for her to operate and fly into airfields which most wide-bodied jets would never use. That is why the airplane was scheduled for both the domestic and the international route web of the company. In spite of this scheduling pattern, the few hours I spent operating the craft were blissful ones, as far as living was concerned. The other side of the coin in operating the craft as first officer (F/O) involved some events that affected particular scheduled flights in the presence of passengers. The presence of passengers on board not only made the events real, but also confirmed the wisdom of incorporating some manoeuvres into the flight simulation proficiency programme. That one is able to write about these events shows how flight simulation is getting closer and closer to reality.

Flight simulation is a sort of "technical elixir" that prepares a pilot for handling an abnormal situation in a real flight. I must mention that events related here in respect of flying the airbus have been selected out of the numerous occurrences that formed part of my active career as F/O on the airplane. The need to select these events stems from the fact that repetition is boring. I have therefore chosen events the types of which I had never encountered prior to my flying the A310 airplane, i.e. neither on the F27 nor on the B737 fleet.

The Events

SUDDENLY WE LOST THE RUNWAY

It was on the 10th of November, 1985. At 6.00 a.m. LCT on that day, the city of Lagos was covered in a blanket of low stratus cloud, which was unusual for the month of November. The morning was dull and overcast as a result. But apart from this, it was just another day, and reporting for duty was business as usual. Flight WT 540 that morning was scheduled for 7.00 a.m. LCT departure. It left blocks on schedule, with all hands on deck to achieve this. The trip was a daily scheduled service on the A310 fleet, for Los–Kan–Miul–Kan–Los with scheduled arrival time back in Lagos as 2.00 p.m. LCT. I was operating that morning with a nice chap of a captain, and the flight was fun all the way. On our return leg to Lagos, the captain delegated the duties of the pilot flying (PF) to me, which made him the pilot not flying (PNF). The last leg was from Kano to Lagos. The operations hand in Kano had given us the Lagos weather forecast for 1.00 p.m. which suggested the likelihood of rain showers around Lagos airport by the time of our estimated arrival in Lagos. I did the flying from Kano. The whole trip was normal until we got the update for Lagos weather. Lagos was now in thunderstorm (TIS) and rain, but with eight kilometres of visibility. From this information, at least one thing was certain: the TIS cell or front had passed Lagos, so everything was okay. Then we descended and finally got cleared for the ILS 19R approach in Lagos. I flew in on the ILS electronic slide slope and azimuth bar which makes things easier during let-down in rain storms. At about five miles ahead of us, we saw the runway and, procedurally, the PNF announced this simultaneously to Lagos tower and to me (the PF). Then we concluded the landing checklist. The rain was there but we could see the runway. Then suddenly, as I was just about flaring the airplane for landing, we got engulfed in the rain and in a jiffy the visibility in the cockpit with reference to the runway dropped to zero. Flaring an airplane is an action of de-rotation that controls the impact of its landing gear with the runway. This action must be carefully carried out first for safety reasons and secondly for passenger comfort. Mastering this skill is a department of its own in the total art of flight execution. Neither the captain nor I could see a thing as we felt the wheels touch the runway. Then the flight got dramatic. For us crew, one thing was certain: we were on the runway. The only question was what part of the runway, or how far we had gone into the runway. Well, in a situation like this, bringing the airplane to a complete stop in the shortest possible time is crucial. So both the captain and I applied all the necessary procedures. We finally came to a stop and still couldn't see a thing. Then what made the drama worse was the communication pause (all through this dramatic period of just eighty-five seconds that seemed a millennium) between us and the ATC hand. He had cleared us to land. It was when he was about to announce to us our landing time that he saw us being engulfed in the rain. But once he couldn't see us any more he just kept quiet. That silence surely gave us the graveyard feeling. Thank God that by the time the rain blew over, we were on the runway centre line, fully stagnant and in one piece with 175 passengers in the cabin who were of course oblivious of the close call.

As soon as the tower hand sighted the airplane again, his communication box crackled into life, announced our landing time and gave us taxi clearance to our parking point. I felt betrayed, but legally he was just doing his job. Flying is science. What you don't see you don't relate to. So as far as he couldn't see us, technically, we had not landed. The bottom line! *This flying business, some business indeed and some way of life.* As a retired United Airline captain used to tell us, "Folks, each time you go up there and eventually get back home, you've cheated death once again." For that frightful moment in this particular flight, death had hung around hoping to collect the backlog of debt owed it, but it had not been forthcoming, thank goodness.

WRITER'S QUOTE:

The recognition of death as a finality when confronted by it is a strong source of strength in trying to overcome it.

Death is a dual phenomenon.

Then We Actually Lost the Engine

The opportunity of flying one of the best airplanes in the Nigeria Airways fleet was really a thrilling experience. One flight path abnormality that most twin-jet pilots all over the world have come to respect, due to their inability to master it in good time and remain consistent with the mastery, is engine loss. Its mastery involves a special manoeuvre which is very important.

The consensus among manufacturers and pilots is that the take-off phase of flight is the most critical for an engine loss. This is simply because, given the deployment at this stage of high-lift surface devices like the flaps and slats coupled with the cumulative weight of the craft, if immediately after getting airborne an engine suddenly shuts down the torrent of events becomes chain-like. First, the airplane's overall thrust is reduced by half. Then all the lift devices (if left too late) quickly become viciously drag-inducing, thereby causing a further rapid loss of speed that would eventually lead to a stall, or in common parlance, total loss of lift, at which juncture the pull of gravity takes over to complete the internment of the flight. Without a positive and spontaneous corrective action taken at this critical phase of flight, in an engine-out condition loss of speed comes as easy as breathing. So would the loss of the equipment and all the souls on board, and in an unlucky situation some innocent souls on the ground also get taken along in the toll.

The nightmare of encountering engine loss at this critical phase, when compared with the B737 airplane, turned out to be a blissful thing on the twin engine A310 airplane. The respite lies in the time factor with regard to the duration of total loss of thrust for the A310 Pratt and Whitney engine. Each engine has a power output of 50,000 lbs of thrust, compared to the B737's 15,000 lbs thrust. I still recall vividly that throughout my flight simulation for this manoeuvre on the A310 airplane I was never at any time found wanting. For any pilot who has flown the B737 prior to flying the A310 (assuming the pilot had mastered the corrective procedure in this instance), this manoeuvre is just a walkover. For me it remained so throughout my career on the A310.

So on the 29th of December 1985, on flight WT 105 from Port Harcourt to Lagos, with 196 passengers on board, panic, fear, and anxiety were completely absent during an engine loss. As a matter of fact, I was the PF when the engine just exploded during take-off and climbing through 6,000 ft altitude. The major reason for writing about this event has nothing to do with getting the airplane back in control, but to describe the theatrical scene that subsequently took place in the first-class passenger cabin of the airplane when the passengers heard the loud bang from the exploded engine. The comedy as reopened by the purser (the head of the cabin) went like this:

The flight was the last one from Port Harcourt to Lagos for the day, and the first-class cabin was full of eminent personalities, mostly from the east with numerous red caps signifying the calibre of people on board. Among the personalities was the president of the traditional medical practitioners of Nigeria. His profession at that time (in the 1980s) generated a lot of controversy because of public scepticism towards the efficacy of their unorthodox methods of drug administration. The eminent traditional medicine personality took off his pair of shoes immediately he heard the explosion from the engine, and placed the shoes directly in front of him. Then (to the utmost surprise of the crew in the first-class cabin) the rest of the first-class passengers took a cue from this man's action. The purser recounted that they did this very swiftly and religiously too. In my response to the story, I told the purser that was just the passenger part of the flying business and an effort in self-preservation. To this day, I still feel quite sad that I was unable to witness this airborne comedy.

We returned en route to Port Harcourt with the remaining engine and made a successful landing.

As for the rest of my career flying on the A310, it was Jimmy Johnson's jingo all the way till my last flight on the 5th of July, 1987, after which I resigned to go into the international job market. The late 1980s saw the country experiencing a difficult economic climate culminating in the introduction of the Structural Adjustment Programme (SAP), which made life very difficult. The corollary was that most professionals in the country ventured into the global job market in search of greener pastures. I too got carried away in this whirlwind for a period of seven months before I got re-engaged with my career foundation company, Nigeria Airways.

Re-engagement advanced me towards the pilot's career goal of becoming a captain. A friend and colleague of mine came to my house one afternoon just to visit. During our conversation, he drew my attention to a (Nigerian) newspaper he had been reading and asked me to read the summation of the news editor on why the Nigerian soccer team failed to win the then ongoing African Cup of Nations tournament. The editor submitted that the

Nigerian Football Association (NFA), before the tournament started, had set up so many committees as the antidote against not bringing the cup home. The NFA had different committees for the players' well-being: accommodation; allowance; the coaches; the fans; smooth passage; etc. After implementing all these, the NFA of course felt that all loopholes had been taken care of and that the rest should be left to fate. It was after the tournament that the NFA realised that they'd omitted one vital committee: they never set up a committee for the scoring of goals!

In the goal of becoming a captain, the committee is only a one-man committee: the candidate himself.

The Making of a Captain

In aviation parlance, the function of a captain is expressed as *taking command*. In the airline pilots' hierarchy, the captain is the most senior. To aspire for the top of one's career is a universal thing. Working towards the achievement of this goal is exciting, but as soon as one gets there, the initial enthusiasm is reduced.

From my experience, I found out (though it did not surprise me) that to be the head, leader or supervisor in any venture attracts a different degree of pleasure and pain, commensurate with the amount of responsibility that goes with the position. Also, becoming a captain in an airline is one thing that has remained flexible so to speak. As for governing aviation authorities globally, it is assumed in theory that any pilot who is over twenty-three years of age and who has logged a total of 1,500 hours of flight time and met certain specified conditions is qualified to undergo training for the certificate of an Air Transport Pilot's License (ATPL). If and when he has passed both the ground and flight phases of this course, he is then issued the ATPL. The possession of this license confers recognition on that person by the authority as a captain.

Unfortunately, in passenger carrier airlines, this certification or endorsement is just a mere proof that the holder has met the governing authorities' standards required for that endorsement. It does not automatically make him a captain, though his possession of the endorsement is highly recognised by the airline. Being made a captain is entirely centred upon the company's policy, and if policy in the ideal situation is a broad decision involving value judgement, then the sub-heading "The Making of a Captain" is entirely the company's affair. But that aviation parlance of "taking command" is entirely an individual thing.

For the individual career pilot, the journey towards "taking command" starts from the date of one's employment. The logic behind this is very clear and simple. As a subordinate or rookie, you take and obey orders, in consonance with the laws governing your conduct in your professional field. From years of research, it has been proved beyond reasonable doubt that learning to obey in the best and proper manner leads to learning the best way to *command*. Any form of inadequacy in this process of servitude leads to a drag in learning to command. An individual aspiring to command must have integrity, which is usually best exhibited in the individual's attitudes. Once offered the command position by his company, the onus is on the individual to attain consummate aptitude in this capacity. Sometimes, he may have to seek help in realising and developing this.

Being offered command by one's company is an integral part in the making of a captain. For the individual, the offer criteria, though tempting and evidence of career plum, should not mislead the individual. Leadership, any day, is *the moment of truth*. More so when it involves invaluable human lives and management of equipment of colossal monetary value.

As for being offered command by reputable passenger airliners all over the western world, primarily the concept of improving consummately over the governing authorities' legal requirement is the basic policy followed. The difference in policy lies in the emphasis in different areas of the criteria that constitute the policy. Factors that lead to this difference in emphasis are so numerous that trying to delve into that will only be a wild goose chase. So the bottom line is "uneasy lies the head that wears the crown".

I earlier on asserted that the making of a captain starts from day one as a career pilot; but becoming one is the prerogative of the company.

Ideally, most commercial airlines put into consideration their recommended candidate's ability, their seniority position on the line for that professional group, with the mandatory command orientation programme forming a major aspect of the whole process. The programme was introduced in cognisance of the fact that the pilot as a professional is a specialised technician. So in taking up the supervisory role he needs to be properly groomed. All the prerequisites I have mentioned have their primary source in having logged the required flight time, which in the case of Nigeria Airways is a minimum of 3,000 hours.

So, in the making of a captain, I shall now go into the details of what is involved, drawing largely from my own personal experience. Towards the end of 1987 (precisely in November), and shortly after I got back from the pilots' global market and got re-engaged by my old company (Nigeria Airways), I received a memorandum, along with four other colleagues, conveying the company's decision that the five of us should move up to the position of captain on the B737 airplane. I was elated at this offer, although it did not come as a surprise to me. I had at that time actively flown as F/O on three different fleets for a period of seven years, with a flawless professional record, and had logged a total of over 4,000 hours. The contents of the memo reflected our course programme and date of commencement. Since the final objective was for us to become captains on the B737, the possession of an airline transport licence was mandatory. The company's memo slated the airline transport licence course (ATP) for the month of February 1988 at my former school, Sierra Academy of Aeronautics in California, USA. It was a six-week programme. For me, the choice of school couldn't have been better. It was from this school that I had come to join the company as a second officer in 1979, so going back to her learning environment was like revisiting home for me. For the rest of the guys, unfortunately, it was not so.

I had left Sierra Academy the first time in November 1978 and returned to Nigeria with the dual qualification of a fresh pilot and a flight engineer on turbojet airplanes, with a flight time of just over 250 hours. But thank God that on getting home I realised that the aviation industry was still young and characterised by a shortage of indigenous pilots to replace the outgoing foreign hands. So here was I, with the rest of my group, going back there after ten years, with a total flight time of over 4,000 hours.

On arrival, I came to realise the process of evolution that the school had gone through. The population had grown and the training facilities had been modernised. Sadly, I learnt from the son of the gentleman who owned and ran the school as president when I was a student the first time that the man himself had passed away. The son was now in charge. He turned out to be the only remaining old face I knew. The rest of the staff were completely new hands. Well, the good thing was that the culture had not changed and the tradition was still intact. So I just flowed easily into the school's training system once again.

In pilot certification, the ATPL is the final one. From here, the licence only attracts type endorsement. In aviation, all academic work stops here. Till the end of one's career it is just a story of transition from one airplane to another. Since the course is the capstone in certification, the governing civil aviation authority, leaves no stone unturned in respect of the fulfilment of the stringent requirements for the possession of this certificate. The candidates for certification are thoroughly assessed to the extent that some of them get irritated in the process. For a long while the whole thing appears unattainable, but with hard work one usually overcomes it. It is after getting certified that one comes to appreciate the need for all the stress and pressure of the process. I recall vividly that on the day I got certified, the moment the check pilot held out his hand to shake my sweating palm after two hours of flight in hell and said, "Congratulations, Captain," I sure felt like one, though the journey to being one on the B737 was still far away. And little did I know then that it was just the beginning of the pleasure and pain. If I had known, I would not have celebrated at all.

The ATP course is basically an advanced course curriculum of all the prior certificates. The bottom line is the emphasis on limitations and margin of error in any of the flight training manoeuvres. The margin is so thin that one wonders why they ever called it a margin. For example, the mandatory margin during a non-precision approach (altitude) after reaching the published minimum descent altitude is + 100 − 0. So zero is a margin. What a joke! The minus is the fail point. On the plus side, since it is safe, your being pardoned is a thing between yourself and the fail-happy check pilot. Throughout the six-week programme, I was convinced that this was indeed the ultimate in pilots' certification.

On successful completion of the course my group and I returned to Nigeria in March 1988. The next phase in our march towards the final goal (i.e. being made captain on the B737) was going through the transition training for the B737 airplane as captain. The regulation of the Nigeria Federal Civil Aviation Authority (FCAA) regarding airplane type endorsement for a pilot or crew member is based on the duty the pilot would be discharging on that particular airplane. In this case, they grouped all airplane type endorsement for all persons performing the function of captain on the particular type as the Group I type while the co-pilots were categorised as the Group II type endorsement. I already possessed the Group II endorsement, so the transition course was more of a refresher-cum-lateral programme, technically for the former and an upgrading for the latter. It was back to ground school again, then flight simulation and the aircraft flight training. It was all the same routine transition chain of events except that, in this case, we were now changing from the right seat (the F/O's seat) to the left seat (the captain's). Subsequently, the flight simulator and airplane type rating check would be conducted on the new seat and position. On completion of the base training check, we got our Group I endorsement on the B737 airplane, which legally authorised our operating as captains on the airplane. The minimum training flight period required for completion of the training by the governing authority in Nigeria was basically six hours, including six landings and six take-offs. That was the minimum required, but remember that airplane handling dexterity varies from one individual to another. Well, I made it on the money! Six hours, period.

So much for that. For the airline business, the emphasis on *safety* as a pre-requisite for profitable operations gives rise to the need for more training. The required minimum flight training period during a rookie captain's line indoctrination (quantified in hours) differs from one carrier to another. Every carrier, after satisfying the authorities' requirements, adopts its own training duration that suits its own requirements. In Nigeria Airways, a minimum line training period of 150 hours is required. The emphasis on safety, coupled with the high level of responsibility involved in being released to operate in the capacity of a captain, is reflected in the training captain's having to go through a three-phase flight check (as opposed to only one for the F/O), and a final check referred to as the VIP check, before being released and confirmed as a substantive captain on the particular airplane. The VIP check was introduced recently by the airline with the objective of streamlining the standard required of a captain in the company's context. To achieve this, during the check the cockpit's composition, apart from the rostered captain and his F/O, includes the trainee captain under check and a senior captain from the company's topmost fleet, i.e. the DC10, as the check pilot. He becomes the final authority for the rookies' release as captains.

I got released in January 1990 (January again) as captain on the B737 airplane. The whole journey had started in March 1988. So I became a captain. Now the question follows: who is a captain?

The Captain

Globally, apart from the administrative personnel, staff in other units of most passenger carrier airlines are uniformed staff. So there is need to describe in detail the uniform of the captain, with emphasis on his tailored rank and how to easily identify it. Different airlines adopt different colours of fabric in the tailoring of uniforms for their staff but the epaulet tailoring that betokens the rank of the captain is always the four-shoulder-striped epaulet, worn on each side of the captain's shoulders. This four-stripe pair ranking is universal in the western world although the colouring of the fabric may differ.

In Nigeria Airways, the four-gold-striped epaulet is adopted. In any flight crew composition the captain is the only individual with the wide four-gold-striped epaulet worn on his shoulders. The purser (the head of the cabin) wears something similar, but the difference is reflected in the width of the stripes. The uniform is designed in such a way that the difference in width between a captain's epaulet and that of the purser is easily noticed. I have gone into the importance of uniforms in flight execution earlier on in the book. This time around, I shall relate an incident that happened locally (i.e. on Nigeria Airways) that further justifies the essence of uniforms and the need for the public to be able to differentiate, at a glance, by reference to the uniforms and ranks, the status of the crew member they may be in contact with at any point in time. It would be futile for me to go into details about the uniforms worn by other units of the airline since that would entail writing another book of its own.

Before I go on to clearly delineate crew rank by following the hierarchical chain, the true life story I am about to relate would show the embarrassment and sometimes disappointment which ignorance of rank identification of flight crews often leads to during flight operations. The airline grapevine had it that some time in the early 1980s there was a Nigeria Airways scheduled London service that usually routed Lagos–Kano–London. The plane had just landed in Kano on her first leg, to embark passengers from Kano to London and also refuel. The flight had departed Lagos on schedule and landed in Kano on schedule too. The comedy ensued during the turnaround formalities on the ground in Kano. The airplane in question was the DC10 with the legal cockpit crew composition of the captain, the F/O and the flight engineer. Since the DC10 is a wide-bodied three-man cockpit crew airplane, the function of airplane refuelling lies with the flight engineer. This the flight engineer does after determining the quantity of fuel needed. The information is then passed to the Nigeria Airways ground operations hand in Kano to pass to the airline's refuellers or the company contracted to refuel the airplane.

While the airplane had parked and the usual turnaround activities were in progress, the cockpit crew had a short respite and the flight engineer, who was supposed to be the most actively engaged hand at this phase of operations, went on his own frolic, and assumed that the refuelling of the airplane did not need to be monitored since the figure had been passed on and the action itself was now routine to the refueller. But fate failed him. The refueller on duty that bright afternoon was a new hand, and also a change of shift had just taken place among the fuellers. The refuelling chap in question needed to be told again the quantity of fuel needed. In order to achieve this, the fuel chap climbed the stairs of the DC10 craft innocently looking for the technical crew. He got on board to enquire about the fuel figure for upliftment. On entering the airplane, he saw standing in his path this hulking well-clad fellow wearing the four stripes resembling the captain's and as far as he was concerned, it was the captain. But he was wrong. The hulk was only the overzealous purser. When the refueller asked him how much fuel the airplane should be refuelled with, the purser promptly told him to top her up (as in topping up one's car with fuel). The fuel chap went back and did just that, and of course drove away on completion of the refuelling. Legally, he had done his job.

A few minutes later, when boarding was almost completed, the cockpit crew entered the cockpit and went about their duties until they got to the checklist item of fuel on board, and indirectly joined the comical cast of the comedy that started from the moment the star of the show (the purser) stupidly turned on the tape. The story had it that the cockpit crew were so thrown that they agreed that the fuel figure reflected on the fuel gauges was erroneous. The captain also tried on three different reading glasses of his before he finally brought himself to announce the fuel figure in the gauge before him. Why? Because if what he saw was real, then they were in for a long and embarrassing delay. Right there, the harsh reality dawned. The airplane had been over-filled with fuel and there was now a weight problem.

There have been countless cases of cabin staff and other uni-formed staff or units with outfits that resemble that of the cockpit crew exploiting the public's ignorance of proper designations to commit atrocities for which the pilot (unknow-ingly and indirectly) sometimes gets punished by society. The remedy is to educate the public on the uniforms worn by the crew. But Nigeria Airways captains can now be easily identified.

The Captain's Role

The captain is always giving orders during flight execution, to which every crew member must adhere strictly. He is, therefore, a commander of sorts. His function as a supervisor is further delineated into the task and social functions. The position of a captain in a government-owned airline like Nigeria Airways is volatile. This is where, after hiding under the blissful and protective canopy of another captain while climbing the ladder as an F/O and rookie captain, he finds himself naked and vulnerable to the torrent of government politics. The captain must be tactful so that his status does not lead him into a nightmarish experience. It is a pain-pleasure thing to be a captain. Since politics involves learning how to live with people in a society and not how the people should live with you, an individual needs to build up his reputation and study the society very well. During the final transition to the position of a captain no course is offered. The captain should therefore strive by himself to understand the culture in which he is operating, the political orientation of the society and other essential components of the environment. If he fails to do this, he is likely to be misunderstood. Indeed, there might be reprisals against him if he misreads or misinterprets his socio-cultural and political environment.

That was my experience. I became drowned in politics. I never knew it could lead to the termination of my appointment by the airline. But it did. My career with the airline ended earlier than I had imagined. However, I take solace in the fact that the records are there to prove that I did my job very well. And for that, I thank God.

Glossary

ADF	Automatic Direction Finder
APU	Auxiliary Power Unit
ATC	Air Traffic Control
ATPL	Airline Transport Pilot's Licence
ATS	Air Traffic Service
CAA	Civil Aviation Authority
CAVOK	Ceiling and Visibility OK
CPL	Commercial Pilot's Licence
CPT	Cockpit Procedure Trainer
DME	Distance Measuring Equipment
EGT	Exhaust Gas Temperature
EN	Echo November
EU	Echo Uniform
FE	Flight Engineer
FL	Flight Level
F/O	First Officer
GNS	Ground Navigation System
HSI	Horizontal Situation Indicator
IRS	Inertial Reference System
LIT	Line Indoctrination Training
NDB	Non-Directional Beacon
PF	Pilot Flying
PNF	Pilot Not Flying
PPL	Private Pilot's Licence

PSU	Passage Service Unit
RMI	Radio Magnetic Indicator
SF/O	Senior First Officer
T/O	Take-Off
VHF	Very High Frequency
VOR	Very high frequency Omnidirectional Range

Printed in the United Kingdom
by Lightning Source UK Ltd.
120119UK00001B/18